Life and Food in the Dordogne

Life and Food
in the Dordogne

James Bentley

NEW AMSTERDAM
New York

The paperback edition of this book carries the following ISBN:
1-56663-514-4

Map by Richard Natkiel Associates

First American edition published in 1987 by
NEW AMSTERDAM BOOKS/THE MEREDITH PRESS
171 Madison Avenue
New York, N.Y. 10016.

First printing.

Published by arrangement with
George Weidenfeld & Nicolson, Ltd., London.

Library of Congress Cataloging-in-Publication Data

Bentley, James, 1937–
Life and food in the Dordogne.

Bibliography p. 177
Includes Index.
1. Cookery, French 2. Cookery—France—Dordogne.
3. Dordogne (France)—Social life and customs. I. Title.
TX719.B3974 1987   641.5944'72   87-20396
ISBN 0–941533–04–2

Contents

Acknowledgments

The generosity of my French neighbours still astounds me. Without the help of many friends from the Dordogne this book could not have been written. I thank them here: Audrey, Joanna and E.-J. Bentley; Henk and May Blydenstein; Hans Boss; M. and Mme Célié and Sylvie; Michael and Adrienne Desplat; Michael and Barbara Emerson; M. and Mme Maurice Jardel; Angela Lambert; Jean and Suzanne Lambert; M. and Mme Véril Henri; M. and Mme Véril Moîse; Andrew and Sheila Rowe; M. and Mme J. Taverne. I need also to thank my editor, Vicky Hayward, for her most remarkable enthusiasm, hard work, shared knowledge of food and history – and laughter.

James Bentley
Turnac, 1986

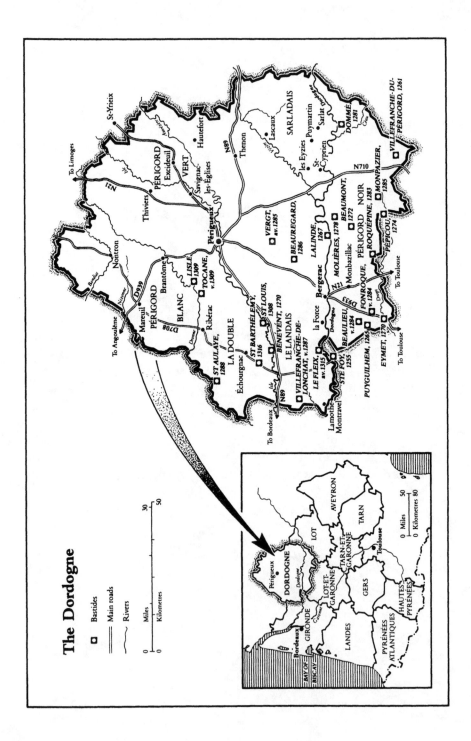

The Dordogne

Bastides □
Main roads
Rivers

Miles 0 ____ 30 ____ 50
Kilometres 0 ____

St-Yrieix

To Limoges

PÉRIGORD
VERT

Excideuil
Savignac-
les-Églises

Thiviers

Hautefort
Thenon
Lascaux

SARLADAIS

Sarlat

les Eyzies
St-
Cyprien
Puymartin

DOMME,
1281

VILLEFRANCHE-DU-
PÉRIGORD, 1261

N89

N710

Nontron

Brantôme

LISLE,
1309
TOCANE,
v.1309

PÉRIGORD
BLANC

Ribérac

Périgueux

VERGT,
av.1285

BEAUREGARD,
1286

LALINDE,
1267

BEAUMONT,
1272

PÉRIGORD NOIR

ROQUÉPINE, 1283

MONPAZIER,
1285

PÉPICOU,
1274

Mareuil

PÉRIGORD

LA DOUBLE

ST BARTHÉLÉMY,
1316

ST LOUIS,
1308

BÉNÉVENT, 1270

LE LANDAIS

MOLIÈRES, 1278

Monbazillac

FONROQUE,
v.1284

Bergerac

la Force

BEAULIEU,
v.1284

N21

D708

ST AULAYE,
1288

Échourgnac

VILLEFRANCHE-DE-
LONCHAT, v.1287

LE FLEIX,
av.1315

STE FOY,
1255

PUYGUILHEM,
1265

EYMET,
1270

To Bordeaux

Lamothe-
Montravel

To Toulouse

To Angoulême

D939

To Toulouse

To Toulouse

DORDOGNE
Périgueux

LOT

AVEYRON

TARN

TARN-ET-
GARONNE

LOT-ET-
GARONNE

GIRONDE

Bordeaux

LANDES

GERS

Toulouse

PYRÉNÉES
ATLANTIQUES

HAUTES-
PYRÉNÉES

BAY OF
BISCAY

0 Miles   50
0 Kilometres 80

Foreword

This book is a sequel to Elizabeth Romer's classic account of life and food in an Italian valley, *The Tuscan Year*. But it has a rather different emphasis. I have drawn more on the literary and cultural history of Périgord, the rich region now enclosed by the *département* of the Dordogne, and I have described the kitchens and ways of cooking of the chefs in the great châteaux as well as those of my neighbours and friends throughout the region. This seemed appropriate to the food eaten here. For, contrary to many people's assumptions, the fine regional cookery to be found today in the Dordogne came about relatively recently, during the course of the nineteenth century. Until then deprivation and starvation marked the life of the Périgord peasantry; their poverty was such that for centuries cuisine beyond bare necessity could exist only in the kitchens of the châteaux and the *traiteurs* who prepared cooked food for wealthy households.

That is the tradition commonly known as *grande cuisine*, or *haute cuisine* – deliberately and consciously refined, codified and passed on through books as well as in the kitchen itself, reliant on the idea of luxury and extravagance rather than necessity. It reflects the romantic legacy of the past – the changing tastes and influences of the great lords who successively ruled the region and, in more recent times, the great chefs and gourmets whose personalities and contributions are individually remembered: this is the cooking of Brillat-Savarin, Carême and Escoffier. Over the centuries Périgord evolved a tradition of such cuisine famed throughout France. Part of the secret lay in the abundance of nature. As André Lamande put it, 'the earth of Périgord is paved with truffles and rendered paradise by *foie gras*.' (And much more too: this is a land also of vines and walnuts, game and river fish.) Périgord has also consistently produced a disproportionate number of the country's finest chefs. Of them all, the most famous was André Noël, who became chef to the king of Prussia in the eighteenth century, when his court was culturally renowned throughout Europe. In our own times, Marcel Boulestin is probably the best known culinary son of Périgord.

The eventual development of a more regional style of cooking resulted from a symbiosis between this tradition and peasant necessity. It came about in several ways. One was a fairly rapid transformation at the time of the 1789 Revolution. Many of the chefs to the aristocracy (and *traiteurs*) were left suddenly unemployed, a shift that had momentous results in culinary history. These were the cooks who became the great restaurateurs, *pâtissiers* and *charcutiers* of the next century. To give just one example, in 1789 the Prince de Condé went into exile. His chef, Robert, opened a restaurant in the rue de Richelieu, Paris. Slowly, he recruited his former colleagues, themselves also thrown out of work by Condé's sudden flight – 'an infinite plethora of young persons, each more talented than their neighbour', as André Carême observed in 1822. In such restaurants, the *bourgeoisie* met to talk and eat, acquiring tastes they wished to satisfy in their own homes, and for this paying clientele the chefs refined and introduced many new techniques and dishes.

Far more gradually, these changes filtered into the homes of the newly wealthy middle classes. Cookery books flooded on to the market to give access to the techniques of a cuisine previously available only to the aristocracy. As the economic position of the *bourgeoisie* improved they also increasingly employed the daughters of the tenant farmers to work in their kitchens, just as the aristocracy had done before the revolution. Thus, the style of cooking also made its way back into poorer farm kitchens, but only as improvements in living standards allowed. Nonetheless, in certain periods these were substantial. During the Second Empire, for example, the people of this class drank three times as much wine as before and ate nearly twice as many potatoes. They also had far greater access to game and fish and, through the enlarging market for the produce they took to market, spare cash to purchase increasingly varied foodstuffs they could not grow – previously unheard of luxuries like sugar and white flour. Thus, a new cuisine began to develop combining the sturdiness of the peasant kitchen with the refinement of *haute cuisine*. Although its ingredients varied according to level of income, it nevertheless had a distinctive style common to the wealthiest and poorer households. At the same time, the policy of centralism being pursued by the Paris government to bring the regions of France under a far tighter rein, and the slow but prolonged depopulation of the countryside, both of which began in the middle of the nineteenth century, gave regional food an important emotional value – along with patois, folklore and other customs previously looked down on because of their peasant origins. This undoubtedly led to a deliberate nurturing of traditional dishes, to new dishes with a traditional feel – and to the myth that many of them had been eaten in peasant homes for centuries.

This is the regional cooking of Périgord we know today, handed on from generation to generation, often by word of mouth – at one level lovingly cherished as the personal memory of what *grand-mère* used to cook in the same kitchen and often on the same stove half a century earlier; at another an almost entirely anonymous popular tradition. It is a living and changing tradition, but still marked by the old rhythms of life – the seasons of the year and the Christian festivals, even though religious belief has declined (insofar as it has ever deeply existed among some sections of the French population). Marriages, transactions over land, funerals and holy days are still usually observed by ceremonial and sometimes excessive feasting.

The regional pride in good cooking can still be felt very strongly today, too. Food is discussed at great length and Dordogne dishes nearly always extolled at the cost of food from anywhere outside the *département*, whether it is neighbouring Quercy, Agenais and Limousin, or distant Paris. The recipes special to this part of France symbolise to the people of Périgord the unchanging skills and patterns of life, a permanent way of looking at the world and its gifts. Over the years, watching my neighbours cook and eating in restaurants throughout the region, I have also become convinced that the culinary skills found on the farms and in the town households are not so far removed from the gastronomic secrets of the finest professional kitchens. This is not so surprising, given the origins of this style of cooking, and I hope that the crossover shows through in this book.

I hope this is not a didactic book. I would not claim to be a fit interpreter of local lore, despite the generosity of my neighbours. Rather I wanted to write a record of one Englishman's sampling of life and food in the Dordogne, acquired by looking, reading, exploring and, above all, tasting. It is a book based on personal research, on learning from my French neighbours, on trial and error in the kitchen, on favourite cookery books and on what I have read in the works of the great gourmets – above all the extraordinary Curnonsky. It is also, of course, based on what I have eaten in the restaurants of Périgord.

I have tried to express a few rules and ways of the people of this region. One is to cook simple food well. Where ingredients are difficult (or expensive) to obtain, I have suggested suitable substitutes for individual recipes. Improvisation around necessity and availability according to your own taste is definitely more in the spirit of the Périgord kitchen. If some of the recipes do not seem very exact by the present-day standards of presenting recipes as precise chemical formulae, that is because the cooking of the Dordogne rarely depends on exact proportions, timing or temperature. But I have given weights and measures where necessary, as they would be used in French shops, with metric to standard conversions in the back of the book for cooks who need them.

Some readers may also be surprised by the inclusion, or exclusion, of particular dishes. A few recipes are omitted, even if they are typical of this region. One of my neighbours told me that he has never known a day pass since he was weaned without a piece of horsemeat passing his lips. For my part, I tend to avoid those butchers who sport a carved horse's head outside their shops. (But beware, too, of the fact that a carved horse's head is not invariably displayed outside a horse-butcher's.) I have also tended to omit dishes which the French themselves would buy from a specialist: *pâtisserie*, *charcuterie* and bread, in particular. On the other hand, I have included some everyday dishes which are not unique to this region, but nevertheless eaten here a great deal.

Finally, the leisurely pace of this book is intended as some sort of recompense for the habit of rushing over food or gulping down wine. Good food deserves respect and understanding.

The Village

'Generations have found here an especially hospitable earth, offering them natural shade, the basic material for their tools, the delicious warmth of the slopes, the abundant water of rivers, the game of the plateaux and plains – a Paradise, or at least a Promised Land.'

MAURICE ROBERT

The stones of the Dordogne are more beautiful than those of the English Cotswolds. Our house is over five hundred years old, at least, and its stones were bound together with earth for mortar. When we first bought the house, these were covered on the inside with an unsightly plaster. Laboriously we chipped the plaster away. We learned from our neighbours the correct mixture of mortar, sand and lime to fill the joins between the stones. And as we worked we learned more and more about our new home.

A local farmer made a delivery of sand just as we were opening up a square, hidden cavity in one wall. He explained that we had discovered the secret hideaway where the treasures of the family would be stored. In our barn we came across a huge, curiously shaped pot, with two spouts: that, he told us, was for walnut oil, which, until the advent of gas lamps and commercial salad oil, was used both for lighting and cooking. Near it lay a curious assortment of chains and strips of metal so puzzling that I was about to throw them away – until the farmer explained that they were extremely precious devices for weighing live chickens, ducks and even pigs.

Later I was to see them still in use at the weekly markets of Périgord.

In that barn, too, we found some roughly shaped pieces of wood, which my wife fitted together into a neat, simple table. Until we visited the national museum of tobacco at Bergerac I did not realise that we had inherited an old fashioned table for rolling tobacco leaves.

Inside the house we discovered old windows, now filled in. Later I learned that the Directory in the late eighteenth century had introduced a window tax, abolished only in 1917. People responded by blocking up their windows. In any case, they reasoned that the fewer their windows, the warmer their homes.

We also rejoiced that the whole length of the ground floor was a wine-cellar. No barrels remained, though many old iron hoops had been left there. The barrels themselves had been supported at one end by a stone ledge built out from the wall, at the other by huge ancient logs. The place was, and is, wonderfully cool, even on the hottest summer day. No doubt once it housed pigs and fowl as well as wine; one door did not reach to the ground, allowing both air and chickens to circulate in and out. Our neighbours did not seem to mind that we intended to convert the room into a huge dining-room and a kitchen. One lent me a power-drill to level the rock floor. Another cut us an impressive length of heart-of-oak, to strengthen our one suspect beam. But though they never said as much, I am sure they felt this showed that the English will never take home-made wines as seriously as a French peasant.

Our greatest discovery lay behind the fireplace, a monstrosity covered with brown-stained wood. To our eyes it was not attractive, so we pulled it down, to reveal an amazing carved stone fireplace, over which was a huge blackened beam. We had uncovered a fireplace, in the *style rustique*, dating from at least the early sixteenth century. Chimneys then were built large and high in order to let people step inside them for cooking and other tasks without bending down. Huge andirons, known as *landiers*, stopped the burning wood from falling out of the hearth. We never use the hooks on our *landiers* for cooking on a spit, but the hooks are still there and were in use until we moved in. A huge chain also hung down the chimney, to hold the cooking pot. We bought a huge metal fireback, made of cast-iron and bearing the *fleur-de-lys* and the salamander, the device of François I, to throw the heat into the room, manhandling it up the path of the village (since the van delivering it was too wide) and finally heaving it into place with satisfaction and relief.

Later one of the villagers would tell us a treasured tale about this fireplace concerning the last owner of the house, Mme Maria, who had died some years before. (He never tires of this tale, nor do we.) Mme Maria, known as *la pauvre Maria* – even though she could afford a personal servant and was highly intelligent – used to sit of an evening in the corner of this huge fireplace, warming herself and knitting. One day the villagers crept to the outside wall with a ladder and a pail of water. They climbed to the chimney and drenched *la pauvre Maria* to her skin. After her initial shock, she seems to have taken the practical joke in good part and, till her death at well over eighty, would happily recount the tale herself.

As if the remarkable discoveries inside our new home were not enough, the village outside disclosed wonders. I am fascinated by the history of my own Dordogne village. Some can be pieced together from the memories of those who still live there; other facts can be gleaned from books and records; others simply from the village itself, and its white-stoned buildings walled against intruders. At the very entrance to the village is a church – tiny, seven hundred years old, and scarcely ever used. (The last time was over twelve years ago, for the baptism of the one boy who lives here.) For fear of thieves, the lovely seventeenth-century carvings of Christ's Passion have been taken away. A post-box, yellow and incongruous, has been fixed to the church door. Opposite is the village graveyard, well-kept, locked, with the plastic flowers in honour of the dead so beloved by the French. Half-way down the lane we discovered an open-air, unused bread-oven. It seems that in the fairly recent past one family in the village would bake bread for the rest on one day of the week, another family taking over the next day, and so on. Before that most families baked rarely and in very large batches, every two weeks and sometimes even at longer intervals. A loaf could weigh up to eight kilos. As a result people mostly ate mouldy bread. A traditional proverb ran, 'A good house stores dry bread and dry wood.'

Life has scarcely been uneventful. Nearby is a cave that sheltered the local priest during the most atheistic period of the French

Revolution. Go through the village, past our house and barn, and you reach a building that was used by the *maquisards* for radio transmissions during World War II. The Nazis caught them. One *maquisard* was M. Véril. He spent the rest of the war in Buchenwald concentration camp, and narrowly escaped death at the hands of the Russians. He does not like snow, he says, because it reminds him of those Buchenwald days. Fortunately we get only a light scattering, even when it falls elsewhere in the Dordogne. Beyond this building, among trees, is set a tomb, possibly of a Protestant who did not wish to be buried in a Catholic cemetery or in the cemetery at the entrance to our village. No-one seems to know who is buried there and so far I have been unable to trace any documentary references to it.

What is clear is that the village in its present form post-dates the Hundred Years' War, when it was completely destroyed. After the Wars of Religion had come to an end, the villagers came back and grew in number. The reign of François I had seen as many as fifteen hearths here. That number seems never to have been reached again; but in the seventeenth century the villagers placed in our church the fine carvings of the Passion. Slowly the village began to prosper, growing rye and oats and grapes. Then, from the middle of the nineteenth century, came a massive decline. Twenty-five years ago nearly every house was in ruins. Only three or four inhabitants, of whom Mme Maria was one, kept the place alive. The historian Jean Maubourget was distressed to find the carvings of the Passion crumbling to dust, gardens overgrown, weeds everywhere, an ancient box-tree one of the few signs that once this village had been loved and cared for.

That was twenty-five years ago. Our village has partly come to life since then. The debris has been cleared away. On old foundations the houses have been rebuilt, especially on the side of the village overlooking the river. 'Perhaps it is an old village that looks a little too new', wrote Maubourget; 'but seen from the other side of the river on the low beach the place has the air of somehow having been there from the beginning of time.'

Our own house never actually fell down. Mme Maria and her servant Élie were two out of the four villagers seen by Maubourget. Both were strong characters. Mme Maria was clearly held in some respect and is still spoken of in that way, which makes me sceptical of certain academics' claims that older women were in traditional society almost universally derided. The demographer Peter N. Stearns, for example, has written of the recent past, and specifically of France, 'women were treated horribly in the popular culture of traditional society: widows past forty-five were not expected to remarry in the village, though a minority had enough defiance, or property, or even good looks to do so. . . .' Certainly, Élie himself was living proof that women past forty-five were not to be spurned. When we bought the house his health was failing. He packed his lifetime's possessions into one small case and went to the splendid old people's home in Domme – a fine hostel, conveniently sited between the church and the graveyard. Three times he persuaded some unfortunate lady he met in the old people's home at Domme to leave and live with him – each time in *her* house. Three times, alas, these women found him impossible to live with. Élie said humourously of one of them, 'She didn't want to turn over the pages of my newspaper for me, let alone make enough cups of coffee to keep me going.' He himself left behind as a gift for us his old metal coffee pot, which had never left the fire during the day.

Élie was an entertaining rogue. I used to enjoy meeting him, in his cap and carpet slippers, the inevitable yellow cigarette between his lips. Once he asked whether he could come and look at what we had done to the house. I am certain that he disapproved, even though he was too polite to say. He did, however, ask why the villagers had put up a 'cul de sac' sign at the entrance to our hamlet. One of his own delights had been to watch motorists who had erroneously driven up the narrow path – it is almost too narrow for a car and certainly too narrow for a tractor with a harrow – desperately trying to turn round without damaging their expensive cars on the thick, stone walls.

I am also certain he was the person Maubourget described as 'an inexhaustibly garrulous expert in manures'. Mme Maria treasured a bed of fine roses and made Élie tend them carefully. The day after she died he ripped them out of the ground. He then grew outside the house a fine hydrangea that is still there, enclosing it with wire-netting, in case (he told me) 'the Parisians' came and stole it.

We were all sorry when Élie died. He had gone to Bordeaux for a serious operation and died on the operating table. To everyone's annoyance the authorities in Bordeaux assumed he had no friends and buried Élie in some public grave. The best that could be done to put matters right was to arrange a requiem Mass, attended by the whole village, in the chapel of the Domme old people's home.

To wander down to the Vérils' house at the bottom of our meadow is to enter another world of memories and rich merriment. There are plenty of excuses for doing so: to buy eggs, or simply to find out how people are faring. My younger daughter, the first time she ever went for eggs, greatly admired Mme Véril's rabbits. To her horror, the next time she went for eggs she found Mme Véril slaughtering one of them. Rabbits are for eating here, not for pets. They also have two dogs, Venus and her mother Dolly, lovely soft animals who come plodding across the field and lie appealingly in my flower beds. Usually they are a source of amusement as well as powerful guard dogs, although they are apt to snap at your hand if you stroke them while their mistress is plucking a duck. Mme Véril paid over seventy francs to put Venus on a contraceptive pill. Venus responded by producing thirteen puppies – put to death by her mistress two days after they were born.

The Vérils are the closest of our neighbours. We are a small village. Just outside the ancient walls live M. et Mme Véril Henri, whose chickens and hens frequently leap across the road just as you are passing. M. Véril's brother, Moïse, and his wife live south-west of our house, where a time-trodden pathway leads through the meadow and a gap in the hedge – a gap wide enough to let pass a tractor and cart. M. and Mme Desplat Michel, with their children Francis and Natalie, live just by the old church as you enter the village. Adrienne Desplat is known for her wonderful *confits*. Then there are the holiday homes. For instance, two Parisian doctors live here. You might think this a bonus, but when I was stung by a wasp as I perched at the top of a ladder replacing a broken roof tile, Dr. Frédérique Dommois, sunbathing in her bikini in her deckchair on her patio, far from rushing across with medical aid, simply shouted, 'Bathe the sting in vinegar', and went on reading *Paris Match*.

It is always pleasant to stop and shake hands with our neighbours should they be around. Like all the people in this part of France, they love to talk, discuss, consider opinions and give views and advice. I always try and persuade them to tell me patois words: for the table, my shirt, the animals. Verbs are conjugated differently in

Langue d'Oc and French and the relationship between the two is far from close. The former is a subtle tongue; on market days stall holders talk to each other in it; brothers and sisters still chatter away in it. And there is none of the brusqueness that one sometimes finds in the big cities.

People often ask me whether you find a welcome or instead some resentment in this region. There is no resentment; there is warmth. The pace is still leisurely. More than that, farmers in each community still know each other and rely on each other for protection and mutual help. So, I am expected to pull my weight within the village, but I am also offered considerable help.

I first felt I really belonged to the village on the day M. Véril Moïse made the remark, 'We must keep your land well stocked.' This followed the never-forgotten incident of the sale of the walnut tree. One of our trees had given up the ghost despite all my attempts to prevent this. M. Véril had suggested that, if we wished, he would bring along a man who would buy it off us, cut it down, pull up the roots and take the wood away. 'When he comes,' he had advised, 'ask for 2,000 francs – at least.' The man came and I asked for 2,500 francs. He offered 1,500. Then there was silence. I stammered out, 'What about 2,000?', but the woodman stuck. Desperately I looked at my neighbour but his face remained totally impassive. He must have realised then how much I had to learn. He offered to give me three seven-year-old walnut trees later in the year, at the right planting time.

And M. Véril still gives me help all the time. Whenever, for instance, he hears of a bargain load of wood for the fire – elm, oaks and other good warmth-giving trees – he lets me know. The load is delivered, half for him, half for me. The truck cannot reach my own house because of the narrow road, so we leave the load at the corner of the village, where – because country people respect each other's property – it is perfectly safe until I need it. When he decides that I need to cut up and stack some more wood, he walks across the meadow and asks if he might get out his tractor so that together we can bring a couple of cartloads from the corner of the village to my house. Naturally I accept this generous offer, put in the form of a request. We store the logs in the barn. 'Stack them on their sides,' M. Véril advises, 'or else they won't dry.'

Likewise, I, too, am expected to help when I can. One day, long after our house was in good order and habitable, there came a knock at the door. Outside stood Michel Desplat and his brother-in-law – a handsome man with a moustache, whom I had often met at week-ends, strolling through the village with his gun to shoot any unsuspecting game he might come across. 'We're going to clear the path from here down to the river,' said Michel. It was clear that I was expected to help. Indeed, it was an *honour* to be expected to help. So I abandoned our house-guests and put on my working clothes. All day long, in great heat, we toiled.

Creepers, brambles, huge dead half-buried logs, partly-grown new trees, were all threatening to obliterate the path down to the river. We lugged them out, chopped them down, fought them till they yielded. It was enormously tiring. Michel, who is smaller than I am, is infinitely stronger. He could perch on branches, cutting off other ones with his chain saw. All the people of the countryside are extremely careful about injuries. Again and again both men would cry '*Attention!*', in case something fell on one of our heads or we slipped down the deep abyss. Michel's brother-in-law; however, repeatedly took up huge logs and flung them down the abyss, shouting a warning only after he had thrown them. Then everyone would laugh merrily. The joke filled me with anxiety. By the time we had finished I was exhausted, covered in sweat, in brambles, in seeds that stuck to my hair. But it was a very enjoyable day, and successful. This little path, which we had cleared, leads at times almost vertically down to the River Dordogne and often I see my neighbours contentedly walking home with a plastic bag containing a fine trout or some other river fish.

In some respects, it is surprising that the path has survived. The Dordogne countryside is extremely fertile. As a result nature, left to her own devices, fights back against our puny attempts to cultivate and control her. Nearly 400,000 hectares of the Dordogne still consist of woodlands and forests. It is wise to drive carefully through them, not only because invariably someone is coming the other way (in theory the French drive on the right-hand side of the road; in practice along these country lanes they drive in the middle, till they see someone in their way), but also so as not to miss any single show of the wild life that abounds in this region or to risk killing an animal at night. Often a bird – a hawk, a buzzard, an owl – will swoop majestically ahead. I think that the air currents between the tall trees mean that these birds cannot avoid flying along the main route carved out by the road, so that for up to a hundred yards you can follow them, marvelling at their grace. If you are lucky, and especially at night, you may come on a fox, loping ahead. Lit up in the headlamps of the car, he will run ahead for several hundred yards before darting through a gap in the hedge, his magnificent red brush flowing behind him. Less able to escape the heedless wheels of the motor car is the badger that frequently scuttles across the winding road ahead of you. Even more at risk in summer are the hedgehogs, crawling from one set of undergrowth to another and unaware of the danger of being crushed to death. Much more agile, and more frequently spotted, is the hare, bounding out of the woods, bounding ahead and then bounding away again.

What I have often seen – with unfailing delight – are the delicate deer of the region. I could not begin to count the number of times I've come upon grazing deer in the meadow behind the main forest road to our village, sniffing the air for the scent of danger but heedless of the occasional traffic not a hundred yards away. A little herd will even occasionally trip across the road, unaccountably at peace in spite of the noise of the car engine.

The special beauty of the Dordogne countryside is due to its variety and luscious vegetation. The grass is green; the river never becomes a trickle; the fruit is plump; nature thrives. This is created by the extreme variations in the weather. In winter temperatures can fall to $-12°C$ and the ground will be covered in frost in the morning. For well over one-third of the year the rain falls (172 days in 1975; 144 days in 1976). Curiously enough, given this rainfall, the chalky plateaux that cover much of the Dordogne are notable for their absence of running water. Instead, the water disappears, to be rapidly absorbed into caverns. Rivers flow underground. But innumerable springs suddenly appear and these underground streams also secretly feed the great rivers of the region: the Dordogne, the Vézère, the Dronne and the Isle. Enriched by the snows and the rains of Western Auvergne and Limousin, and by the massifs of Mont Doré, le Cézalier and Cantal which remain snow-covered from December to March, these rivers rise startlingly fast when the snows of the Massif Central are melting, and then they readily flood.

You know it will rain in February. Eugène Le Roy wrote a

charming account of the country year in the Dordogne called
L'Année Rustique en Périgord. Describing the month of February he
uses one telling sentence: '*Il pleut, il pleut, il pleut encore, il pleut
toujours.*' Frequently in winter, as I drive from Carlux to Grolejac, I
have to turn back and find a longer route because after a day or two
of heavy rain the Dordogne has overflowed the road before Saint-
Julian-de-Lampon.

What is never certain here is exactly when spring will come.
Officially it arrives on March 21st, but, as Le Roy observed, 'it is
often late, like the swallow; and in this uncertain season winter
sometimes aggressively returns.' When the weather is bad during
Holy Week, he recorded, the people remark that it, too, is lament-
ing the death of Jesus. Yet the late rain is welcome. 'We want it in
April,' said Le Roy. 'The cattle like it in May.'

For in summer it is very dry. It can be very hot too: the
temperature can reach over 35°C. We swim in the river, or lie on its
banks reading, careful not to lie too long in the burning sun.
Occasionally in the middle of August for a whole day it rains,
sometimes with lightning and thunder. Then the weather is
immediately transformed, and we go swimming again. Often in
the morning the deep valley of the River Dordogne is filled with
mist. The day brings a gentle transformation. The sun creeps
round the house, slowly driving the mist away. If I have to work
outside, now is the time to dig or mix some cement, before the day
becomes too hot. Then the sun beats on our south wall, warming
the yellow stones to such a degree that long after nighfall – even
after midnight – we can sit outside on the terrace, still warm,
chatting, gossiping, musing, watching shooting-stars and man-
made satellites without feeling the slightest hint of cold. Below lie
hectare after hectare of fields that have been cultivated and then left
fallow and then cultivated again; camp sites for tourists; little
houses nearly invisible when the leaves are at their thickest; a
rickety tractor burning smoke in the distance; sheep, following
each other, apparently aimlessly, from one end of a pasture to
another. It appears a completely tranquil landscape. Sometimes, I
can also hear strains of typical French accordion tunes drifting
across from the Véril's farmhouse. M. Véril is often telling me he is
no virtuoso but the music is always agreeable. He invariably plays
his accordion when his son and daughter-in-law come for an

evening. They live in the town. The farm is no longer a family farm, and the son has no intention of taking it over in due course. It is typical of a widespread phenomenon throughout this whole region. The old peasant-proprietor is disappearing. In reality, the landscape is one of long-term crisis.

The statistics are alarming. In the Vézère valley alone an average of thirty-two smallholdings a year are abandoned. The 1200 or so still being farmed in 1954 had been reduced to 700 fifteen years later, and they are still disappearing. The census of 1970 revealed that a good half of the farmers were aged over fifty-five and that many of them could name no future successor. Meanwhile the peasants continue to vanish: 69% of the active workforce in 1954, 37% in 1968, today only 26%. My own commune, Domme, sheltered 1,823 persons in 1876. Today fewer than 800 live there. Villages that once thrived are almost deserted. To take three typical instances, the population of Saint-Vincent-le-Paluel between 1876 and 1962 fell from 372 to 123; that of Sarrazac fell from 1,343 to 823; that of Saint-Amand-de-Coly from 944 to 354.

The crisis is not confined to the Dordogne or to France. But with such an enormous land area – as large as Britain, West Germany, Belgium and the Netherlands put together – and only 53¼ million inhabitants, it shelters far fewer persons per square kilometre than any European country save Spain. There are simply not enough people to farm all the land. Whereas in 1948 France possessed 5 million active farmers, this number had fallen to fewer than 2 million by 1977.

To some extent the crisis has been staved off by bigger farms and more machinery. In 1948 French farmers owned only 100,000 tractors; they owned 1¼ million thirty years later. But for the most part large farms are still confined to the Paris Basin. Attempts to reconsolidate are flying in the face of a longish tradition of doing the opposite. Rationalisation and amalgamation has scarcely touched Périgord, or indeed many other regions of France. What makes matters worse here is that the population is even sparser than elsewhere. The average density per square mile in France is eighty-three persons, but in the valleys of the Dordogne and the Vézère it is scarcely more than forty. Frighteningly, it continues to fall.

In our neighbourhood the closest market is that which takes place at Domme each Thursday morning. But the most important is the

Saturday market at Sarlat. When I first visited the Dordogne in the
month of August I erroneously imagined that this celebrated
market was essentially a tourist affair. Certainly, much there
delights the tourist. Algerians sell trinkets, leather goods, bangles
and belts. Waffles and the ubiquitous thin, salty *frites*, far removed
from the British chip, pungently tempt one's taste for junk food.
Rubber dinghies, straw hats and swimming gear are presumably on
display for those who have left at home such essential holiday
equipment. Sketch artists flatter British schoolteachers and Dutch
bankers spending their summer holidays here. Live *écrevisses* are
bought as playthings for ten-year-olds and tormented to death.
Even the live geese, chickens and ducks seem no more than an
unusually charming backdrop to the countless photographs and
home movie cameras recording annual vacations. Certainly, the
farmers who bring in cheese and poultry are not likely to be buying
the English paperback novels for sale on the open-air bookstalls in
the Place de la Grande Rigaudie and the Rue de la République.

Yet Sarlat market is still a bustling social and commercial
occasion on Wednesday mornings and Saturdays of December,
when there is scarcely a tourist in sight. The sketch artists have
gone, but the Algerians are, surprisingly, still there. So are the
waffle-sellers, joined more recently by stalls offering instant food
claiming to be Vietnamese. But these are peripheral to the men and
women who bring their produce to Sarlat market – and to every
other weekly market in Périgord – who turn up unfailingly, winter
and summer, with good humour, still sporting their berets and
sometimes clogs.

For these markets, and the less frequent fairs, are essential to the
Dordogne economy. They developed in the 1830s in large numbers
throughout this region, largely because the enhanced fortunes of
the *bourgeoisie* made them demand more and more farm products.
Whereas in the past the peasants would bring their butter and cheese
to market maybe once every two months, now it was in their
interests to come every week. The money they earned in this way
meant that other traders found it worthwhile to set up stalls selling
clothing, meat, fish, shoes. As living standards rose among the
peasant farmers the less frequent fairs flourished, dealing in
agricultural tools, other utensils and even cattle. Fairs became
agents of social change, so that, for instance, when the wooden

swing plough was replaced by the so-called '*dombasle*' model in the mid-nineteenth-century it was able gradually to make its way even into remote and backward Périgord. A yet greater change was brought about when wooden ploughs were replaced by metal ones in the second decade of this century. Before then those who lived on the inhospitable higher reaches of the Dordogne were obliged to make annual forays to the richer valleys, picking chestnuts for the farmers lucky enough to be able to grow the great trees that the hilly regions could not support. Now they could buy equipment capable of ploughing some of the rougher lands. Throughout the year the market became the weekly rendezvous of neighbouring villagers, a place where they gossiped, courted, drank a little, exchanged news and ideas, ate and also made money. It is this tradition that feeds the tourists' imaginations today – and their stomachs too, for an army of restaurateurs sprang up in these centres to care for the needs of those who had travelled a long and sometimes cumbersome way to sell and barter.

So, for instance, Cherveix-Cubas, north of Hautefort, began to hold a regular fair on the first Monday of each month. It still does. An important centre like Bergerac regularly sold farm produce on Wednesday and Saturday each week, and animals on the first and third Tuesdays of each month. It still does. Some fairs became noted for specialised products, such as the wickerwork baskets and furniture at Ribérac, still sold every Wednesday from May to September. In less important spots old markets still flourish, and larger fairs remained profitable, though rarer. So, to give one example, each Wednesday people gather for the weekly market, at Piégut-Pluviers, twelve kilometres north of Nontron, and on the Wednesday in the second week in September they turn up for the annual fair.

In some places, the markets and fairs merely spread beyond the confines of far older covered halls – like that you can still see at Cadouin, for example. At Monpazier the beautiful market square, surrounded by cool arcades where in summer you can today sip a glass of wine in the shade and admire the covered hall on the south side, still preserves its ancient measures for weighing out corn. It dates back to the thirteenth century. Monpazier is just one of no fewer than twenty-three new towns, called *bastida* in contemporary documents (from the old French *bastir* to build) and now called *bastides*, founded between 1255 and 1316 in this region. Not all were absolutely new. Domme, for instance, the *bastide* which for centuries protected the hamlet in which we live, was constructed on the site of an older, much smaller town. But they all were set up in response to the turbulence of the age: the first eight belong to the most tense era of the war between the English and the French, another ten were built between 1281 and 1288 when the English held sway and the rest were set up during the Gascony wars between 1294 and 1303. Most were built either for the King of France or for his enemy the King of England, but occasionally a group of individuals would form an alliance to build their own town and see to their own safety.

These new towns proved enormously beneficial to the surrounding countryside. Farmers could work in comparative peace and security, even when devastation was the lot of the rest of Périgord. The Italian poet and statesman Petrarch, visiting France in 1361 saw everywhere 'solitude, desolation and misery – fields deserted and houses ruined and empty, save in the walled towns.' The measure of independence and legal rights, the ability to sell, circulate and trade and the possibility of exploiting new territory attracted many enterprising men and women – who were, in turn, more prosperous customers for what the farmers could grow and breed. Every new town was granted its own market and the centre of each was laid out with its own market square and covered market hall. Thus, the busy, sparkling fair which throngs Monpazier on the third Thursday of each month has, like many others, a far longer tradition than the nineteenth-century markets.

And throughout the region today the farmers still take in to their local market towns once or sometimes twice a week cheese and chickens, geese and *foie gras*, fruit trees, crockery and clasp knives. Every Friday Mme Véril prepares for the market at Sarlat. The chickens and ducks which follow her greedily as she takes them their daily rations unwittingly meet their doom on this day. And on the same day Mme packs her eggs and plucks her fowl, standing in the field, surrounded by the dogs. The next day we will always meet at the market itself – we buying the choice seasonal vegetables and taking a glass of thin beer or more potent wine, she selling the produce she prepared the day before.

It is wandering round the markets that one begins to understand the culinary reputation of Périgord and the fecundity that has contributed so much to it. In one corner a farmer's wife will be selling no more than a handful of ducks. On the opposite side of the market square a hundred live chickens await buyers, who will carry them away head downwards. Beef is often sold on the market. So is cheese. And as the seasons bring their changes, an extraordinary array of locally grown fruit and vegetables appears for sale. In summer, there are strawberries from the Vergt region and the margins of the Barade forest; asparagus from the fields of the Double region; pears and plums from the fruit trees bordering the river beyond Bergerac and long, fine *endives* – the very best kind of chicory, forced in cellars and bleached. The natural produce of the Dordogne countryside, gathered together at the market, still, I must confess, delights and amazes me. Sorrel, asparagus, broad beans, shallots, chives, button onions, garlic, salsifies and the many different salad greens appear as naturally on the market stalls as they do in the menus of this book. In season you can buy mushrooms such as *cèpes* and *girolles*, the early shoots of rocket and dandelion, and shelled walnuts and hazelnuts.

Succulent fresh walnuts are one of the most characteristic ingredients of the Périgord table. You can buy them still in their shells. But the traditional way here is to break the shells and sell the kernels, whole, for cooking purposes. Peasants still sit with a hammer, contentedly cracking walnuts, rejoicing in firm nuts – some of them possibly unaware that this region produces more walnuts than any other part of France. And today they are big business: in the southern part of the *département* Belvès specialises in them; at Doissat, still further south, is a walnut museum. But Terrasson, in the Nontronnais, has grown especially rich on them. There are very many varieties of walnut, which thrive in different conditions of land and climate. Farmers select the right varieties and supply the markets accordingly. We pick ours or, if we can, shake them from the trees at the end of September and the beginning of October.

You may also find *huile de noix*, walnut oil, on sale. It is now becoming widely available as a subtly flavoured salad oil. But in this region it has been used for centuries: farmers still sometimes have their own presses. Now most of the walnuts are sold to be exported as oil, but they are first shelled in the old way – cracked by hand with wooden mallets. Most people in the Dordogne would prefer to use walnut oil rather than butter in almost any recipe. In fact, walnuts turn up everywhere. They are sometimes eaten marinated in the juice of grapes and seasoned with salt and pepper. They are chopped coarsely for salads, or with fresh fruits. But to my mind they are most delightful in a delicious cake.

To make **Miel et noyers** put 250 grammes of clear honey in a large basin in a saucepan of hot water, so that it softens down. Away from the heat pour over it six egg yolks which have been beaten. Add slowly a teacup of sifted plain flour, a teacup of ground walnuts and a little caster sugar. Bind this mixture together with a little cream. Fold in the beaten six whites of egg, and pour the entire mixture into a soufflé dish. Cook for forty minutes in a medium oven. When cold, turn the cake out.

When you are grinding walnuts, if you are using a blender or food-processor, be careful not to over-heat the nuts which will result in the oil separating from the ground kernels.

As the autumn comes, so, too, do two of the most characteristic ingredients of this region: chestnuts and the shiny brown or fawn *cèpes* – flap mushrooms – which take their French name from the south-western patois for the large berets worn by the men. This is only one of Périgord's superb mushrooms. The imperial *oronge*, as yellow as an egg yolk, peeps through dry woods in summer. The delicate *mousseron* grows in the meadow in spring and autumn. The yellow *girolle*, with its delicious smell, shows through in the summer forest. In April and May the curious *morille*, with its pock-marked head, grows on the edges of woods and parks. *Coulemelles*, *rosés des prés* and a black and blue mushroom that is edible in spite of its frightening name *trompette-des-morts*, also appear along with the only mushroom the British know well, the humble but extremely useful *champignon*.

None of these mushrooms would I dare try to cook or eat without first begging one of my neighbours, or a pharmacist, to tell me that they are really edible. It is always necessary to be careful about identification and preparation, and cooking with them is therefore no light task. Certain risks are simply not worth taking. Naturally this goes especially for *trompettes-des-morts*. This dark, trumpet-shaped fungus contains all sorts of slimy grubs and snails, and needs careful cleaning. Most chefs use them only for seasoning. In any case they are happily rare! *Morilles* are constructed of ridges with deep, honeycomb-like pits and need several washes in changes of water before all the earth and grit sticking to them can be removed. They should never be eaten raw, but – like the 'fairy-ring' *mousserons* – are delicious sliced and sautéed. It should be added that the work of preparation is always well rewarded.

Superb as these mushrooms are, they often tend to be overlooked for nature's greatest gastronomic gift to the people of Périgord: an ugly black subterranean tuber called a truffle. Truffle-raising occasions much anxiety here. Often called the 'black diamond of Périgord', prices are absurdly high because fewer and fewer Dordogne farmers produce truffles. An annual crop of ten tonnes a year is not enough to satisfy demand. Yet despite this region's reputation for producing the finest quality truffles in the world, there is no serious endeavour to encourage an industry beyond research to try and establish why the growth of truffles can be linked to truffle-oaks and hazelnuts.

The season for truffles begins in November and you can still readily buy them the following March. I would not begin to try to characterise their taste – though their smell is immensely invigorating. Their shape and size varies, from that of a baby's hand to a child's fist, perhaps two inches in diameter. They appear on market stalls and (canned) in wine shops and *charcuteries*. Since they are so expensive, tourist-orientated shops in Domme and Périgueux offer the cans in string bags, hoping to sell to the visitor what many local inhabitants now deem too expensive. If you bring some home, remember that the contents of a partially used can may be deep-frozen and kept for up to three months. Out of season, the people of Périgord buy truffles dried and freshen them up by soaking in Madeira.

Today the grades of truffle are carefully regulated. In declining order these are (for both preserved and fresh truffles): '*extra*', '*premier choix*', '*deuxième choix*', '*truffes en morceaux*' and '*pelures*' – the latter being skins which are sometimes quite adequate for flavouring a sauce. I would also recommend concentrated truffle essence, *jus de truffes*, which, bought in cans, is easily taken to kitchens elsewhere and keeps well. It is available internationally in delicatessens and speciality food stores. The *truffe du Périgord*, or *Tuber melanosporum*, has neither roots nor stalks nor leaves, but simply grows as a tuber underground, attaching itself to various oak tree roots, but only when the humidity of the ground is right and the soil contains calcium carbonate or limestone. Truffles give off a distinctive scent, but since they lie eight or so inches underground, only a specially trained pig or dog can sniff them. In the past Dordogne truffle-growers would train pigs to dig up the tubers, but then a fight often took place between the farmer and the pig as to who would keep the truffle. Today most growers use dogs. Eagle-eyed farmers can also spot where truffles are likely to be found because bronze-coloured midges (the *Helomyza tuberivova*) often hover just above them.

Since truffles grow in the wild, they are fair game for thieves. So many truffles seem to be stolen in Périgord these days that many a conversation consists of hearing plans to cut down truffle-oaks rather than let the thieves get away with the crop. Near Boulazac a friend of ours has a house among such oaks, which he visits only five or six times in the year. One year, discovering that all his truffles had been stolen and strongly suspecting one particular neighbour, he decided to call in the local police. The policeman visited the neighbour, ascertained that he had indeed stolen the truffles, and came back with a proposed solution: the two men should share the crop.

'Why should I take only half my truffles?' expostulated my friend.

'Well,' the policeman answered, 'you won't actually receive half. Your neighbour will probably divide them up two-thirds for him and one-third for you. That is if he is feeling generous. But at least this way you will get *some* truffles, whereas now you get none. And again: your neighbour is the best man for miles around at finding them. This is a good bargain from your point of view.'

So my friend gave in.

And he does these days collect quite a few truffles from his marauding neighbour. With these he cooks splendid truffle omelettes, one of the classic dishes of the Périgord.

&

For an **Omelette aux truffes** to serve four people you
need 75 grammes of diced truffles, 1½ tablespoonfuls of
goose fat, a dessertspoonful of cognac, a small glass of
Monbazillac, eight eggs, salt and pepper. Put the truffles
in a saucepan with the salt and pepper, half the fat, the
cognac and the Mobazillac. Cover and cook slowly until
the liquid has all evaporated. Beat the eggs and add to
them the truffles, away from the heat. Warm the rest of
the fat in a very large frying pan until it is very hot. Add
the eggs and truffles, pushing in the sides until the
omelette sets. Then roll it out on a hot plate and serve.

If you only have a smaller pan, make individual omelettes. It is
essential that there is only a thin layer of egg for it to cook evenly.

There is a second food you will find on the Dordogne market
stalls which equals the truffle in fame and the eulogies it calls forth:
'a pure marvel of the culinary art', declared Curnonsky, 'a
masterpiece that has assured the glory of our country.' He was
writing, of course, about *foie gras*, now regarded as one of the
greatest gastronomic delicacies and known best to most people in
the rich *pâté* of the same name. The Reverend Sydney Smith
described his idea of heaven as 'eating *pâté de foie gras* to the sound of
trumpets.' In the Dordogne, which is considered to produce the
finest *foie gras*, he would have believed himself to be half-way there.

Although renowned throughout western *haute cuisine*, this rich
liver was until the age of Louis XIV a country dish, unacceptable in
court circles. The trick, however, had been known for centuries.
An ancient Egyptian bas-relief depicts a goose being force-fed. The
Greeks took up the technique. Initially the secret was kept in France
only by Alsatian Jews, but such a secret was bound to be discovered
and adopted by Christians. Rabelais wrote of a monk who used to
swear 'by the patron saint of those who force-feed geese.' The *foie
gras* industry in Périgord, which began as a serious endeavour
between 1810 and 1820, continues to grow; around Sarlat, in
particular, factories produce tins of fine *pâté de foie gras* for export
throughout the world.

Close by our home live no fewer than 9,000 geese, perhaps the
largest single gaggle in the whole of the *département*. Occasionally

they break through their wire fences and wander among the bathers in the river. As you drive through the maize fields and then through the orchards where the geese live, they come rushing up to the fence as you pass, clucking and gobbling away, curious to see what you are doing, idiotic, doomed. Their fate seems melancholy. Although classically made from the livers of geese, these days ducks, too, are increasingly reared to give *foie gras* to an increasingly discerning public. But throughout the whole *département* geese are reared for this purpose, and in the last few weeks of their life force-fed with warm maize to enlarge their livers by as much as six times. There is much dispute about whether or not this force-feeding, known as *le gavage*, hurts the geese, but they appear not to mind and are otherwise usually free-ranging.

Force-feeding the geese lasts three weeks, perhaps a few days more – and four weeks for ducks. I think the birds enjoy becoming involuntary gluttons. Certainly they waddle up contentedly for their turn to be over-fattened, and originally they fattened their own livers by gorging on figs. There are still lots of figs growing here – wild around the rivers, or cultivated, in private gardens and professionally, for sale, dried, on the markets. But maize was adopted for force-feeding geese in the eighteenth century. The maize is always warm, with exactly the right measure shuffled down the fowls' throats.

In late October and early November our neighbour Michel Desplat devotes himself to this task and this alone. Formerly women force-fed geese, sticking the bird between their legs, pushing a funnel down its throat, pouring in boiled maize and stroking the goose's neck until it swallowed the food. Now equality of the sexes allows Michel to take part as well. He is brilliant at the work, dealing with eighty geese an hour, force-feeding each one three times a day. At Sarlat market in the weeks before Christmas and the various *marchés aux gras* held in the region, you can see the result on sale: geese livers the size of plucked chickens and much the same shape. Since maize was adopted for force-feeding, a *foie gras* has been a rich ochre-yellow in colour. It is supple, not too fat, slightly fruity to smell. The best ones weigh between 600 and 800 grammes. On the markets you buy *foie gras* in various forms: '*au naturel*'; '*semi-conservé*', either plain or *truffé*; as *pâté* or '*terrine*' (sometimes dubbed '*suprême*') and often in whole pieces surrounded by pork *pâté*.

There are, of course, many elaborate recipes for *foie gras*. Here, in the land where it is produced, however, it is usually eaten simply, always served at the beginning of the meal and not, as elsewhere in France and at official banquets, at the end. 'Its very richness demands that it be served at the start of the meal,' judged Curnonsky, 'when the appetite is fresh and joyful, and not at the end when the stomach is overfilled with other foods.' Another valuable guideline invariably followed by the people of Périgord, is that it should never be accompanied by a salad: the vinegar would clash with it. This advice was first given to me by a *restaurateur* at Bergerac and intially surprised me, but it makes perfect gastronomic sense. When I find *foie gras* served as part of a very rich main course in restaurants elsewhere, I always think of the way it is served in country restaurants here – with *jambon* as part of the *hors d'oeuvres*, or magnificently alone, to be eaten smeared on a chunk of bread.

Seigneurial Extravagance

'Périgord is one of the regions of our land where
for centuries one has eaten best.'

CURNONSKY, PRINCE ÉLU DES GASTRONOMES

'It is manifestly contrary to the laws of nature,' concluded Jean-Jacques Rousseau in his *Discourse on Inequality* in 1754, 'that a handful of people should gorge themselves with superfluities while the hungry multitude goes in want of necessities.' Looking at the food at the Dordogne inevitably plunges us into social history, a history of resentment and bitterness, self-indulgence and deprivation. For the symbiosis between peasant care and seigneurial extravagance which accounts for the renowned gastronomy of the region arose from conditions in the past which acutely exacerbated man's inhumanity to man. The thousand or so châteaux and manors and the many *gentilshommières* – the homes of country squires, dignified by a corbelled tower or an ornamental doorway – in which the *haute cuisine* of Périgord was created, speak of a romantic past, but they should also remind us of social inequalities, of wealth side-by-side with extreme poverty.

And the contrast between life in the great châteaux of Périgord and in the wretched dwellings of the poor was of course grotesquely reflected in the difference between what the rich and poor ate. Eugène Le Roy, the greatest novelist of the Dordogne, wrote his finest book, *Jacquou le Croquant*, at the end of the nineteenth century, and set its hero, a poor peasant, against the background of the Barade forest. Here he describes how the impoverished Jacquou and his mother look enviously into the kitchen of the château de L'Herm on Christmas Eve, 1815:

'My mother went to light our lantern at the kitchen fire, the open door allowing us to see the great lights within, at the foot of the tower staircase. What a kitchen! On immense fire-dogs of forged iron burned a huge fire of six-foot logs, before which was roasting a fat turkey-cock, stuffed with truffles, which smelled deliciously. On the mantel of the chimney a specially made rack carried half-a-dozen spits with small skewers arranged according to size. Hanging on boards fixed to the walls saucepans of all sizes shone in the reflexion of the hearth, above enormous kettles and basins, which gleamed like polished gold. Moulds of red copper and pewter stood on little tables, where there were also other strangely-shaped utensils whose purpose we could not guess. On the long heavy table knives were set out according to size on a napkin; and we saw, too, wrought-iron boxes with compartments for herbs. One of the two grills was loaded with puddings, the other with pig's trotters, ready to be placed on the spit which a scullery-maid was turning in the corner of the chimney. On this table, too, stood slices of cold meat and pâtés in their golden crusts.'

When they return home there is little for supper but a *mique*, or corn meal ball. 'Poor boy,' exclaimed Jacquou's mother. 'There's nothing decent here . . .' But, taking the lid off a pot, she added, 'Here's a meal ball for you.' 'As I was eating this corn ball,' Jacquou remembered, 'kneaded with water, cooked with cabbage leaves, without even a scrap of lard in it, and completely cold, I was thinking of all those good things that I had glimpsed in the kitchen of the château, and I do not deny that it made the *mique* seem a poor affair – as indeed it was.'

It is not so much the real threat of starvation, but this sense of forbidden access that creates the focus of discontent. The sense of injustice that burns through Le Roy's novels was drawn from personal experience and first-hand observation; his father's family had served the lords of Hautefort, the greatest baroque château in the whole of southern France, for generations and his mother was chambermaid there.

His fictional account is more than borne out by contemporary sources. Even as late as the early nineteenth century, peasants of this region, save perhaps around Bergerac, never had the wherewithal

to make even the simple dishes like *miques*. Most of them were, as
one witness put it, 'like wandering skeletons, scrabbling vegetables
out of the ground'. What made their lives still more miserable was
that a good many of them were obliged to give up most of what
they managed to cultivate to the great houses whose tenant-farmers
they were. This lasted long after the end of the *ancien régime* in 1789.

Yet while many starved the wealthy enjoyed sumptuous self-
indulgence. Beauvillier's treatise *L'Art du cuisinier*, 1824, which
became a standard work of reference, suggested a typical menu for
dinner. He set out the dishes in two columns. They included:

Soup:
    onion soup   *consommé*

Second course:
    roast beef or mutton   a *daube* of turkey

Entrées:
    cutlets   topside of veal
    chicken with cucumber chicken *en lézards*
    veal sweatbreads   lasagne
    young rabbit and eels   fillet of sole
    fillet of beef   casserole of veal
                      sweatbreads

Roasts:
    quail   pigeon
    lamb   capon

Entremets:
    gâteau   carp

To this gargantuan menu Beauvilliers added two salads, peas,
lettuce, cauliflower and artichokes, as well as biscuits, *gâteau*, *crème
aux pistaches* and apricot fritters.

This grotesque contrast can be traced back through the centuries.
Fernand Braudel quotes a chronicler of late sixteenth-century Aix-
en-Provence, who describes the distribution of bread to the poor:
'in the crush of the said poor, six or seven persons died, children,
girls and a woman, having been pushed to the ground, trampled
and suffocated, for there were more than 1,200 poor people there.'
The evidence of superfluity at other levels of society at that time is

evident in the châteaux themselves. Go round any great château in the Dordogne – Biron, Beynac, Salignac, Les Bories – and you find huge kitchens, with cupboards that once groaned with provisions and silver salvers. Some of the Dordogne châteaux possessed as many as ten rooms set aside for preparing food: kitchens, cabinets, rooms for keeping meats, other rooms for chickens, yet others for geese, store-rooms for crockery, cellars for wine, as well as a bakery. The dining-rooms became more and more ornate, with carved ceilings and expensive tapestries.

It is in the dominance and control of these châteaux and the massive churches which served as fortresses as well as houses of prayer that the roots of the enduring inequality lay. The injustice involved in the feudal tenancies under which a lord exercised extreme political and social control over a number of communities is symbolised architecturally, just as the superfluity of diet is represented by the scale of the kitchens. Nearly always the châteaux dominate strategic points and grandly look down on the villages below. Take château Hautefort, for example, with its massive walls, its twin round towers, both of them double-domed, and its ornamental garden. As you drive from Limoges into Périgord, it dominates the little village of Hautefort. A medieval fortress stood here in the twelfth century, if not earlier. This was the home of troubadours and of violent men of war, sometimes the same persons. All that remains of the old fortress is its drawbridge. The present arrogant (and splendid) building dates from the mid-seventeenth century, built from 1640 onwards for the miserly Jacques-François, *seigneur* of Hautefort.

Countless other such examples stud the landscape. There is the magnificent château of Beynac, which once ruled one of the four baronies of Périgord – the others were Mareuil, Bourdeilles and Biron – and across the river the huge château of Castelnaud. Then there is Montfort, perhaps the best known, which changed hands and was rebuilt several times during its turbulent history. Nearly every strategic point was controlled in this way. At Piégut-Pleuviers the majestic keep of the castle that dominated the road south into Périgord remains; at Limeuil, where the Vézère joins the Dordogne, the powerful château still looms over gently sloping streets and medieval buildings. Finally, the picturesque village of Issigeac, south of the River Dordogne, which the Bishops of Sarlat long ago made into their summer home, is a reminder that the lords were spiritual as well as temporal.

From these castles, palaces and manor-houses, the nobles ruled the countryside, levying taxes along the rivers and, sometimes, roads. Those who set up the *bastides* also profited since they claimed the right to tax those who moved into them. And they also directly controlled food supplies. The nobles of Guyenne claimed the game of the woods and ancient forests – the forest of Ligueux, the forest de Born near Hautefort, the forest around Vergt, and the great Barade forest south-east of Périgueux – as their own and rigorously enforced poaching laws. The peasants stole and used what they could. The monarchy itself tried to regulate fishing, delegating authority to the great ones in their châteaux alongside the rivers. The laws were regularly disobeyed. Court records from the past abound in cases of fighting between fishermen and the servants of the great ones. Peasants continued to claim ancient rights. They poached at night, on Sundays, during *fêtes*; they fished with prohibited methods and lines. They even thumbed their noses at the authorities by fishing under the very walls of the châteaux. They broke the boats of the notables and sometimes protested by stopping all river traffic altogether.

Yet the lords were able to exercise extraordinary control through the feudal dues they levied on the produce of their tenants' lands. They literally controlled the landscape for their own purposes. At Bassilac, close to where the River Isle meets the River Auvézère, stands the Château de Rognac, built in the sixteenth century by Henri IV's almoner. He rerouted the river that ran by his new home. His successors built a mill next to their château, to grind their corn freshly on the spot.

Through this control and at an appalling cost to their tenants developed the seigneurial extravagance common to all regions of France. There are indications, however, that the cuisine of Périgord was already considered particularly fine. The warlike troubadour Bertrand de Born felt sufficiently incensed that so many noblemen preferred good living, fine food and drink, to making war that he complained about their preference for eating so much that they skimped on fighting equipment and soldiery. In the sixteenth century, Henri de Navarre, the future Henri IV of France – who later became famous for his declaration that everyone should have a chicken in the pot – was given hospitality by Michel de Montaigne. The cuisine so impressed him that he set about obtaining the services of a Périgord chef – Buade de Saint-Cernin, who had learned his trade in the château de Saint-Cernin-de-Labarde.

In part, the quality of cooking was created by the richness of the earth and the geographical position of the region: the cooks had access not only to the game and fish which the nobles claimed as their own, but also to the fruits and vegetables of the fertile, well-watered soil. As early as 1384 Pope John XXII, who had been archpriest of Sarlat and a canon of Périgueux but was obliged to leave Périgord and live at Avignon, decided to plant the right sort of oak trees there in the hope of having truffles always on hand. This was also an area of rich dairy and beef pastures and, lying in the hinterland of the great port of Bordeaux, was supplied by river with the luxury foodstuffs of other countries and climates: spices, sugar, wines. The wealth generated by Bordeaux, particularly during the English presence in the area, was felt throughout the region.

Paradoxically, the upheavals of war also contributed. Bertrand de Born might complain that his enemies 'ravage my land, burn my crops, smash down my fruit trees and mix my grain with the straw.' No doubt this made *haute cuisine* difficult. But war also brought new masters, swift changes in the patterns of people's lives, social mobility and the spread of ideas – including ideas about cooking. It also brought new foodstuffs. Invading Romans brought chestnuts, geese, *foie gras* and probably also the vine. The Hundred Years' War made Bordeaux a rich port, whose wealth and imports filtered through the whole region (these included, after the discovery of the New World, the all-important maize and the less-important but still significant tomato). During the Wars of Religion Bergerac became a Protestant stronghold and developed a wine trade, a trade which outlasted the extreme passions of the sixteenth century.

Today, it is still possible to recognise in menus some of the dishes which we know were served and eaten centuries ago by the Dordogne nobility and which have come down to us through the chefs of the great houses. On 20 January 1450 Gabriel du Mas entertained at Périgueux the Archbishop of Narbonne, François Lord of Biron, and many notables and canons of Périgueux, to a huge feast. To feed everyone, we are told, du Mas had to borrow every scrap of silver belonging to the *seigneur* of Ladouze. They consumed, successively; wine as an *apéritif*; veal liver in sauce; two sorts of soup (one with chives); roast capon served with little lampreys; mutton with capers; teal and game; kidneys; rabbit; *brochet* of partridge; two hams, cured differently; a wild boar, set among chestnuts; pastries; milky puddings; plums and cream; pears soaked in wine and sugar; fruit tarts; and much red wine. Certain of the characteristics of the medieval and, more particularly, the Périgord table, already stand out clearly. The long succession of meat and game dishes, many cooked on an open fire, is typical of that period. So, too, are the *compôtes de fruits*, which were often cooked in red wine. These are still very popular in the Dordogne, usually made with strawberries, cherries, plums or pears.

This is how some of the most distinctively regional dishes on Gabriel du Mas's menu would be cooked in the Dordogne today.

> To prepare **Foie de veau aux oignons** you need two soupspoonfuls of flour, a glass of dry white Bergerac, a soupspoonful of vinegar, four onions, chopped up parsley, a sprig of fresh tarragon, 50 grammes of goose fat, salt, pepper and four slices of veal liver. Wash and cut the onions into four quarters. Lightly flour the liver slices. Warm the fat in a frying pan. Sauté the onions lightly in this and then add the liver slices. Turn them over and cook until done, making sure the interior retains some pinkish hues. Take the slices and onions out of the pan and keep them warm on the serving plates. Deglaze the pan with the white wine; add *bouillon*, the chopped tarragon and the vinegar. Season, cooking for a couple more minutes, before pouring this sauce over the liver slices and onions. Serve sprinkled with parsley.

Rognons de veau is on the menu of countless restaurants in our vicinity. Most of them, I guess, slightly compromise with the traditions of Dordogne cooking and use a little butter. Marsala is also used instead of Madeira, which is an essential ingredient of Périgord food.

&

For **Rognons de veau** for four people allow 2 large veal kidneys. Cut the fat off the kidneys, skin them and remove any hard bits. Chop into slices. Chop an onion and fry it in goose fat. Add 250 grammes of sliced mushrooms, followed by the kidneys, adding more fat if necessary. Salt and pepper and cook for five or six minutes. Add a large glass of Madeira and simmer for another four or five minutes. Take out the kidneys and put them on a serving dish. Keep warm. Reduce the sauce and then pour it over the kidneys before serving, garnishing with chopped parsley.

If you wish to wash the kidneys, place them whole in boiling water with lemon juice added; leave for 4 minutes, remove and drain.

The kidneys were followed by rabbit. At Bergerac I was once served a tender *lapereau*, served with prunes that had been cooked in local red wine. The dish is typical of medieval tastes for unexpectedly sweet sauces served with meat and game. In fact, it originates from the neighbouring département of Agen, where wonderfully moist, plump prunes are a speciality and used in all kinds of dishes.

&

Choose a young rabbit, weighing about 1½ kilos for **Lapereau aux pruneaux**. Joint it and season with crushed thyme. Warm some goose fat in a casserole and then sauté the pieces of rabbit meat in it over a hot stove. Take them out, season them and spoon off the fat from the casserole. Put back the rabbit along with a diced onion, three diced shallots and a ladleful of stock. Add three crushed cloves of garlic, cover, and cook gently for half-an-hour. In another pan swell twenty prunes in 500 ml of red Bergerac, adding 50 grammes of sugar, a little water, and then heating (though not boiling) the syrup. Take out the rabbit and place the pieces on serving plates. Keep them warm. Put the prunes into the casserole, with a glass added of the liquid in which they have been swollen. Heat for a few minutes. Take off the heat. Add 200 ml of cream, stir well and then pour over the rabbit. Serve.

In those days, the forests were filled with far more large game than today and it would not be unusual to find on the menu of a medieval Périgord banquet *marcassin, chevreuil, moufflon* – young boar, venison and wild sheep. If you see these words on a menu in Périgord today, you are lucky indeed. A survey published by the hunters' Fédération revealed that in February 1980 the wild boar of the *département* comprised only about one hundred beasts. About two hundred stags roamed in Périgord *noir* and Périgord *vert*. Between five and six hundred roe wandered chiefly in the Double and Barade forests. And around the Auvézère were counted about thirty *moufflons*.

The forest between Grolejac and our own village is supposed to be the haunt of wild boars. In fact, a large number of them live behind a tough electric fence here, bred both for food and also to delight the week-end hunters. I must confess, however, that I have never seen a wild boar out of captivity in all my walks through these woods and during any of my countless car trips from our village to Grolejac and back. Wild boar frequently disappoints those who try to eat it. The only way properly to cope with the toughened older animals you are more likely to find than the *marcassins* is to casserole them. *Daube de sanglier* is a delicacy, provided that it has been cooked for a long time, quite slowly, until the flesh has become tender. On the rare occasions I have eaten it in the Dordogne it has been served with a delicious purée of chestnuts – exactly the same combination presented at Gabriel du Mas's banquet.

Chevreuil, venison, is eaten more often. After a successful deer hunt venison is still often simply roasted on a spit. Often, too, you can find saddle of roe.

Selle de chevreuil is wrapped with *lardons* and then marinated for two or three hours in two tablespoonfuls of fat, a spoonful of cognac and another of white wine, parsley and a sliced onion. Salt and pepper the saddle, and then either roast or fry it.

If you wish to try these recipes with less expensive and more easily obtained meat, lamb is probably the best choice. In France it is considered the closest in flavour and texture, particularly with the help of a marinade.

A more sophisticated method marinates the meat for two days before very slow cooking in an earthenware pot.

For **Cuissot de cerf** take 1¼ kilos of venison. Make a cooked marinade with a medium-sized sliced onion, a chopped carrot and a small stick of celery. Sauté these in a little fat or oil for about five minutes and add a clove or two of garlic, two bay leaves, thyme, ground black pepper and a little salt. Pour half a bottle of red wine into the pan and simmer the marinade for about twenty minutes. Remove from the heat. When it is cooled, pour it over the meat. Leave the venison in the marinade for two days, turning morning and evening. To cook the meat, take it from the marinade and remove any pieces of vegetable sticking to it. Brown it in hot fat, and put it in an earthenware pot. In the same fat fry a sliced onion and a sliced carrot. Put these into the pot. Pour over the strained marinade, and add 2½ cupfuls of water, some sliced mushrooms, pepper, a little salt and a clove of garlic. Over the top of the venison put a thick piece of ham fat. Cover the pan with a tight-fitting lid, and let the liquid just come to the boil. Let it cook very slowly, preferably in a low oven, for about 3½ hours.

The people of Périgord would not eat such a dish without making an accompanying tart cherry sauce. This would also be good with roast duck.

While the venison is cooking, prepare a **Sauce aux cerises**. Take the stones out of a cupful of fresh, preserved or tinned cherries. In a small pan dissolve two tablespoonfuls of red currant jelly. Add the cherries and a little of their juice (if there is any), a pinch of black pepper, a teaspoonful of wine vinegar and a dessert-spoonful of coriander seed. Simmer for five minutes.

Fifteen minutes before serving, put all the liquid and the vegetables from the venison through a sieve. Keep the meat hot (cover the pan). Rapidly boil the cooking juices to two-thirds of their volume. Add this to the cherry sauce and pour the whole back over the meat.

Alongside the large game would always be the smaller birds like *perdreaux*, *cailles* and *faisans* – partridges, quail and pheasants. These birds are very often roasted, still traditionally *en brochet*, skewered on a spit.

A **Perdreau rôti** is well-seasoned with salt and wrapped in bacon – the bacon should be lean. After roasting it is often served on a croûton that has been fried in the fat of the partridge and then covered with cooked cheese.

Quail is still traditionally poached rather than roasted, which keeps the flesh moist.

For **Cailles à la périgourdine** you need four quail, 100 grammes of raw chicken breast, a finely copped shallot (only a tablespoonful), a tablespoonful of oil, four tablespoonfuls of breadcrumbs, one tablespoonful of finely chopped bacon, thyme, salt and pepper, 600 ml of game stock and two tablespoonfuls of Madeira. Sauté the shallot lightly in the oil. Stir in the breadcrumbs. Finely shred the chicken breast and stir that in too, along with the bacon. Cook for three or four minutes. Keep stirring. Season with the salt, pepper and thyme. Then stuff the birds with the mixture. Quail can be fastened up with a wooden cocktail stick. Add the birds to the stock, which should be boiling. Reduce the heat and poach for fifteen minutes. Add the Madeira to the stock for flavouring the birds.

Sometimes these are served *à la gelée*: that is cold, in a game aspic made from the cooled stock. I have also seen recipes in which the stuffing uses *foie gras* and truffles, but this is not the original version.

Sugar cane was introduced to France in the thirteenth century, but it remained a luxury of high social prestige until the eighteenth century due to its expense. One of the most sumptuous desserts of this region is a *crème de châtaignes* served rather like the better known *Mont-Blanc aux marrons*, but with different flavours to both the chestnut and chantilly *crèmes*.

♣

Crème de châtaignes is made with a kilo of chestnuts, four packets of vanilla sugar, 750 grammes of granulated sugar, four soupspoonfuls of Monbazillac or other sweet white wine, three soupspoonfuls of icing sugar, 250 ml of fresh cream and twelve pieces of sponge cake or biscuits. Put the chestnuts into the water, bring to the boil and cook for about thirty-five minutes. Remove the skins and put the pulp into a liquidizer or processor, or through a sieve. Put the granulated sugar and vanilla sugar with three soupspoonfuls of water into a casserole. Leave to simmer until the sugar is dissolved. Add the purée of chestnuts and cook for five minutes, stirring all the time so that the mixture does not harden. Remove from the heat and leave to cool. Rinse a Savarin ring under cold water, but do not dry it. Pour in the cream of chestnuts and chill for twelve hours. The following day pour the Monbazillac on to a plate and soak the sponge cakes or biscuits in the wine for two hours. Crush the biscuits into a *pâte*. Whip 250 ml of cream into a chantilly with three soupspoonfuls of icing sugar and the biscuit *pâte*. Mix together gently. Empty the cream of chestnuts on to a plate and put the chantilly cream in the middle. Chill it for two hours before serving.

The medieval taste for marzipan sweetmeats can still be sampled today in the *confiseries*, where walnut halves stuck together with almond paste and prunes stuffed in the same way are sold by weight. They were more likely to appear on menus than pastries until later medieval times when the art of the *pâtissier* developed considerably.

All tarts need **pâte sucrée**. On to a cool work surface sift
100 grammes of plain flour with a pinch of salt. Cut 50
grammes of butter into small cubes, and then put it into a
well made in the middle of the flour, along with one egg
yolk and 25 grammes of caster sugar. Work in the flour
with your fingers, blending in the fat and egg until well
mixed. The dough is then kneaded for a few minutes
until it becomes a small ball. Before using, the dough
must be placed in a polythene bag in a refrigerator for at
least thirty minutes.

For a flan case, the pastry should be rolled out thinly, using icing
sugar to prevent sticking, and baked blind, covered with waxed or
greaseproof paper and weighted with beans. (Some people use
washed and dried cherry stones, which give off a wonderful
aroma.)

One of the best fruit tarts is *aux fraises*, the flavour of the
strawberries combining beautifully with a vanilla *crème patissière*.
Strawberries were first introduced into France in the thirteenth
century, but now they are cultivated everywhere and *tarte aux fraises*
is found throughout France. Today, however, you can be fairly
certain that wherever you eat it, unless it is made with *fraises de bois*,
the strawberries have come from this region. Several parts of
Périgord have taken successfully to cultivating strawberries, and
Vergt, in particular, bids fair to become the major strawberry
market of France.

For the filling of a 200-mm **Tarte aux fraises** hull 400
grammes of strawberries. Wash and drain in a colander.
Boil 250 ml of red currant jelly, two tablespoons of
granulated sugar and two tablespoonfuls of cognac in a
small saucepan. (It is ready when the drops off a metal
spoon are sticky.) Thinly coat the interior of the shell and
leave to set. This prevents the biscuit-like pastry soften-
ing. Save the rest of the glaze for the strawberries. The
Crème patissière is made by blending two eggs, 50

grammes of vanilla sugar and two tablespoons of plain
flour, in a large bowl. Bring to the boil 300 ml of milk
and pour on the egg mixture, stirring continuously.
Return to the pan and bring the mixture back to the boil,
stirring all the time. Immediately remove from the heat
and stir in 25 grammes of unsalted butter. Cover with
damp greaseproof paper and allow to cool. Spread the
crème patissière over the base of the pastry shell. Arrange
the strawberries on top of the cream. Spoon over the
glazing.

Perhaps the only surprising omissons from Gabriel du Mas's menu,
particularly to the gastronomic eye, are dishes with truffles and *foie
gras*, since these are now the foods most commonly associated with
Périgord. Indeed, within the canons of *grande cuisine*, *à la Périgourdine* almost invariably implies the use of truffles or *foie gras* as a
garnish, or flavouring to a sauce or stuffing. Despite their expense,
it would be unfair not to give these recipes – and, in particular, to
suggest through the recipes themselves how their use transferred
from the domestic kitchen to that of restaurant kitchens across the
world. The recipes and techniques must have first become known
outside the region through aristocratic and ecclesiastical patrons
who took their chefs abroad. In the eighteenth century, for
example, André Noël, who was born at Périgueux in 1726 and died
in Berlin in 1801, became chef to the king of Prussia shortly after
Voltaire was at the court there. A contemporary drawing depicts
André Noël in knee-breeches, periwigged, a parasol under his arm,
walking delicately with a cane. He has the ample stomach of a true
son of Périgord. Then, too, the cookery books that began codifying
cuisine, particularly from the seventeenth century onwards, started
a pattern of exporting and internationalising originally regional
food.

The single best-known and widely cooked recipe from this
tradition of Périgord cooking is *sauce périgueux*, now an essential
ingredient of many dishes and part of the repertoire of every French
chef. It is often, mistakenly, called Dordogne sauce, *sauce périgourdine*, which obscures its origins in the capital of Périgord. In
culinary terms, it is very similar to a Madeira sauce with the
addition of truffles.

&

To make **Sauce Périgueux** you need goose fat, half a cupful of white wine, three tablespoonfuls of cognac, a sliced onion, three chopped shallots, three truffles, a tablespoonful of beef stock, a tablespoonful of flour and salt and pepper. Fry the shallots in some goose fat. Add the wine and brandy and ignite. In a different pan lightly brown the onion, adding a little beef stock. Prepare a *roux* with more goose fat and the flour. Stir in the onion and shallots with their liquid and simmer over a very low heat for an hour, stirring frequently. Season with salt and pepper. Dice the truffles into small pieces. Strain the sauce, add the truffles and reheat for a few minutes.

Here, the best substitute for truffles would probably be mushrooms with a little truffle essence used for flavour. In other recipes, there is little point in trying to find a substitute.

&

For **Perdreau truffé**, for example, you need 100 grammes of fresh bread, sieved, 80 grammes of peeled truffles, cut into quarters and seasoned with salt, pepper and a glass of cognac. The partridge is stuffed with these, wrapped in fat bacon and cooked for about thirty-five minutes, traditionally on a spit.

Other far more elaborate dishes clearly have the same roots as these simpler versions from home kitchens. There is a recipe for stuffed quail, for instance, with a far richer stuffing and sauce, but essentially the same flavours.

&

To make **Cailles farcies à la truffe et au madère à la sauce périgueux** you need, for four persons, eight quails, eight strips of bacon (cut off rinds and keep), 250 grammes of chicken or duck livers, 250 grammes of

champignons, three soupspoonfuls of butter, two glasses
of Madeira, a small onion, one sliced truffle and some
truffle skins. Chop and mix together the livers, the bacon
rinds, the *champignons* and the onion. (This can be done in
a food processor.) Then melt half the butter in a frying
pan and add the blended mixture. Cook for two or three
minutes. Salt and pepper it well. Take out of the frying
pan, and then add the Madeira. Stir well. With this
mixture stuff the quails. Into each bird place an eighth of
the truffles, and then wrap each one in the bacon strips,
tying them up. In the rest of the butter sauté the quails
until they are golden, moistening with more Madeira
and letting them cook for about twenty minutes. Make
the *sauce périgueux* according to the recipe on page 40.

In the same way, rich stuffings combining *foie gras* and truffles can
be seen both in recipes reflecting the regional origin of the
combination and the far more refined dishes adapted to impress
with other luxury ingredients. A goose's neck can be brilliantly,
spicily stuffed, transforming something the British would undoubtedly throw away into a succulent delicacy.

&

For **Cou d'oie farci**, cut fresh *foie gras* into pieces and
finely chop 25 grammes of truffles. Put into a mixing
bowl 500 grammes of sausagemeat; add the chopped *foie
gras* and the truffles. Test the seasoning and leave
overnight. Next day, fill the goose's neck with the
stuffing. Roast gently in goose fat for 1½ hours. This can
be eaten either hot or cold, cut like a sausage. If you wish
to keep it till a later date, it can be preserved in the goose
fat for three or four weeks. Make sure all the air is
excluded. Sometimes sorrel is also added to the stuffing.

Again, there are more refined recipes in which the regional
origins of the dish are not so clear.

A **Perdreau farci** is stuffed with a forcemeat made from
chopped truffles, breadcrumbs, *foie gras* and the livers.
The birds are sautéed in a casserole, when you should add
some chopped garlic, more sliced truffle (if you can
afford it) and a glass of cognac. The casserole is now
sealed, and the second half of the cooking takes place in
the oven.

Another rich dish typical of Périgord is *filet de boeuf sarladaise*, in
which the fillet is served accompanied by toast spread with *foie gras*.
The traditional spit-roasting, the use of the toast rather like the
old-fashioned bread trenchers served under roast meat, and the lack
of ornate presentation suggest this is a very old local dish which was
simply taken into the repertoire of *grande cuisine* due to its
gastronomic appeal.

For **Filet de boeuf sarladaise** for six persons you need a
kilo of fillet of beef, two truffles, strips of bacon, a glass
of dry white Bergerac wine, twelve thin slices of bread,
100 grammes of *foie gras* and 300 ml of *sauce périgueux*.
Stick in the fillet some cubes of bacon and then wrap the
whole with fatty bacon strips. Stick pieces of truffle at
regular intervals over the whole, using wooden cocktail
sticks. Cook the fillet on a spit, over a hot flame. You
pour the wine into the dripping pan and from time to
time use this to moisten the fillet. While this is going on,
toast the bread and spread with *foie gras*. Arrange this
bread around the serving dish. When the fillet is cooked,
remove the bacon, cut it up and add it to the dripping
pan. Skim off the fat and add the juices to the *sauce
périgueux*. This should be served in a gravy boat while the
fillet is served among the toasted bread.

Other dishes using both the truffles and *foie gras* are clearly the
more elaborate creations of chefs. Invariably called *à la périgourdine*,
to my mind they are not really as typical of this region as simpler
dishes like a truffle omelette or *cou d'oie farci*. In this category I
would place the following recipe.

&

For **Truffe en chaussons**, also known as **truffe en croûte**, place some slices of *foie gras* on puff pastry. Season truffle slices with salt, wrap them in slices of fat bacon and place on the *foie gras*. Fold over the pastry till it makes a wallet, brush it with egg and bake in a hot oven for twenty minutes.

In the larger version of this dish, *truffe tourte à la périgourdine*, the truffles and *foie gras* are sprinkled before cooking with cognac and Madeira.

&

Another such dish is **Oeufs à la périgourdine**. For six you need half a dozen hard-boiled eggs, 150 grammes of *foie gras truffé*, some chervil and chopped parsley, salt and pepper. Cut the eggs in half lengthways, remove the yolks and mash these with the *foie gras truffé*, the chervil, parsley, salt and pepper. Then press the mixture back into the egg whites.

To my mind these are not a great improvement on plain stuffed eggs. Far more delicious and unusual are the hot truffled eggs of this region. *Oeufs truffés* are, again, made with *pâté de foie gras truffé*, not simply with truffles – which does make them an expensive treat.

&

To cook six **Oeufs truffés** you need 125 grammes of *pâté de foie gras truffé*, another two egg whites, a cupful of breadcrumbs, salt and pepper, chervil and parsley. The eggs should be boiled until hard, shelled and then cut in two crosswise. You slice a little of the white off each end, so that they can stand up on a plate. The yolks are then mixed with the *foie gras*, the parsley, chervil, salt and pepper and used to stuff the egg halves. Beat the extra egg whites and put them in a soup bowl. Roll each of the stuffed egg halves in the egg whites, cover with bread-crumbs and leave to dry for a few minutes. Then plunge

the eggs into a frying pan filled with hot goose fat. Take
the eggs out when they are golden, remove surplus fat
with absorbent paper and serve hot.

These dishes may seem very extravagant. Yet they are an intrinsic
part of the food of this region, if only cooked occasionally on special
occasions or eaten out in fine restaurants. It is also salutary to
remember that – as with oysters in England – there was a time when
both truffles and *foie gras* were not highly esteemed and were eaten
by the poor. To my mind, it is these recipes that are best – nothing
can surpass a simple truffle omelette.

The Generous Earth

'This man, although poor, is happy because he has
no artificial needs, because a little is enough for him
and because he is free.'

EUGÈNE LE ROY

Over thirty-five years ago Philip Oyler wrote a book about the
Dordogne which he called *The Generous Earth*. He prefaced it with a
stanza from Dryden, which begins:

> How happy in his low degree,
> How rich in humble poverty is he
> Who leads a quiet country life,
> Discharged of business, void of strife . . .

All this is dangerously close to the misplaced city-dweller's notion
of idyllic pastoral life. In reality, life is still hard for the farmer and
farm-labourer, and it was far harder in past centuries. When part of
my barn fell down, I asked Michel Desplat if he could help me to
put it up again for a proper rate of pay. Using that elegant French
phrase *en principe*, he replied, 'In principle, yes; but just now I am
totally overworked.' And indeed, many farmers are overworked
for much of the year.

It is the logic of this reality, rather than the myth of country life,
that French regional cookery does not, as many people believe,
embody age-old culinary tradition. When I first read the opening
statement of Georges Rocal's book on the food of Périgord, a

legendary study though written as recently as 1938, stating clearly that it is wrong to think that the peasants and villages of the *département* preserve cooking skills from centuries ago, I was extremely surprised. Rocal insisted that cooking in humble homes was an art developed very recently.

Yet of course he must be right. Peasant communities quite simply did not have the wherewithal to produce gastronomic finery until this century. Their fate was distressing. They lived off red cabbage, chestnuts, the rape which we normally think fit only for livestock, and fruit. They drank either very cheap wine or insipid water. Throughout the centuries the great lords, and the lesser gentlemen too, rigorously enforced poaching laws to prevent the poor living off the abundant fish and game. Rents were high. Under the laws of the *ancien régime* peasants were obliged to give up a large part of their own crops and wines to their superiors.

One study, by Olwen H. Huften, singles out the life of the Dordogne poor in eighteenth-century France as 'an economy of makeshifts'. Jacquou le Croquant and his parents, the creation of Dordogne novelist Eugène le Roy, writing of 1815, counted themselves fortunate to live on chestnuts, potatoes, boiled corn meal and hard, coarse rye bread. Among the poor, game and fowl, meat, milk and eggs remained virtually unknown.

Gradually, the lot of the rural poor improved. After Napoleon the nobility returned, but not the worst excesses of the old *régime*. The poor insisted on new rights, which they clung on to dearly. Of great importance in Périgord was the new right to hunt. Improved communications also led to changes. This vast territory possessed no good roads until the Second Empire; but the coming of the *diligences* opened up Périgord, brought wealth and led to contact with the towns. Children were slowly better educated. Feasts and fairs brought the opportunity for making a little more money, which allowed the amelioration of the peasant table. *Confits* enriched the peasant diet – though not, for a long time, fresh meats. The lesser nobility, who had at times been little better off than the peasantry, began to prosper. There was a demand for reasonably priced hostels and increased demand for farm produce. Birthdays, 'reunions', church feasts became occasions for eating and drinking better.

But it was not until much later in the nineteenth century that substantial improvements could be felt. As an indicator, bread continued to be a luxury and the habit of batch baking in communal village ovens seems to have lasted longer in Périgord than in most other parts of France. Bakers shops were established in the more accessible parts of France in the 1880s, but in the Dordogne they did not appear until well after the turn of this century. By then the people of Périgord were still mainly eating bread made not from flour but chestnut-flour. In 1844 the government had re-introduced hunting permits, which once again threatened the peasants' hard-won privileges. It was as much the early twentieth, as the late nineteenth, century that saw major improvements in everyday diet, largely thanks to railway transport and improved preserving.

The level of resentment is shown by the fact that castles were frequently pillaged; in times of upheaval such as 1848, the gentry looked to defend their halls despite the network of local loyalty. Not surprisingly, the villagers also kept alive the memories of injustice and legacy of petty tyranny for a very long time. According to the historian Eugen Weber, the bitterness lingered especially in Périgord: 'the old songs of 1793 voicing the peasants' resentments of rich farmers and messieurs were revived in 1848 and still sung in 1909.'

I think certain qualifications are necessary to all this. I have no doubt that *some* culinary skills were developed by the poor. Red cabbage, one of the staple foods, ought not to be despised. If you see *chou rouge* on a Dordogne menu, you will usually be offered a satisfying dish which would have existed well over a century ago: cabbage shredded raw and then stewed with a little ham and bacon in goose fat. Sometimes, no doubt also, the poor peasant would manage to poach a partridge from his lord's game reserves which explains, I think, why this bird is sometimes served *au chou rouge* – roasted and then placed on red cabbage. For centuries, too, the daughters of peasant and tenant-farmer families worked as servants in the great houses of Périgord, preparing food under trained cooks and chefs. Nevertheless, a fruitful symbiosis between the cuisine of the great houses and the careful husbandry of the peasant farmer could only develop when the standard of living improved after the extreme poverty of centuries. Rocal is not alone in his view. Louis Stouff, who studied Provençal cooking, came up with a very similar conclusion: namely that 'traditional' dishes were largely an

invention of the nineteenth and twentieth centuries. In particular,
olive oil rather than pork fat was until then used only for eggs, fish
and frying beans.

Today, gastronomically, we profit from this sad economy. The
philosophy of the Périgord table is 'waste not, want not'. Simple
things are cooked well, using the centuries-old traditions of the
kitchens of the *grands seigneurs*. But nothing is thrown away.
Take, for example, the boiled beef left over from a *pot au feu*. It will
be turned into a very fine hash, mixed with chopped onion, garlic,
thyme, a bay leaf, parsley, and heated in *bouillon* to make a cheap,
satisfying meal. Many local butchers do not think it beneath
themselves to follow this housewives' parsimony, so they cook
such a hash and sell it to perceptive customers. Similarly, any left-
over livers are carefully kept in country kitchens. Diced, they are
mixed with sausage meat and cooked in fat for an hour or so, before
being served with a gravy made from veal.

Many Dordogne peasant families can for the most part still
happily subsist on what they themselves produce throughout the
year. The average farmer likes subsistence farming, where he
grows most of what he eats, where as few francs as possible change
hands and where the tax inspector is held at bay. He possesses no
more than thirty-five acres of land, and still prefers polyculture to
the risk of growing a single intensive crop – which may, of course,
suddenly drop in price if the market is flooded after a good harvest.
In many small properties, enough for two pairs of oxen to cultivate
in times gone by, a farmer and his family still grow in strips and
parcels a remarkable variety of vegetables and fruit, and raise their
own chickens, ducks and geese, while the rivers and forests are still
stocked with the fish and game they were forbidden in past
centuries. The philosophy is, not surprisingly, unsentimental. The
earth generously offers a vegetable; then we must cook it. A huge
resource of game roams the forest; it must be hunted and eaten.
Birds strut in the farmyard; they must be fattened, and every morsel
utilised.

The everyday dishes of Périgord share the characteristics of most
peasant cuisines: the economical use of meats; broth and soup as a
filling dish or even a meal in itself; endlessly varied ways of using
those foods which are locally abundant. In this sense, the cookery of
the Dordogne is unusual and, I would say, rises above many other

regional cuisines because it is blessed with such a generous soil. The truffles and mushrooms, locally produced wines and walnut oil, as well as the river fish and forest game, are all still plentiful enough to appear cooked unpretentiously in everyday dishes. And they share with dishes deriving from the great houses the flavour of goose. Whereas elsewhere in France cooking is almost invariably done in butter, here fat is used: duck fat, but above all goose fat. Thus, wrote Curnonsky, Périgord cooking is 'sans beurre et sans reproche' (without butter and irreproachable).

Goose fat is infinitely preferable to pork fat, since it does not go rancid so speedily and its flavour is much lighter. But these days rendered-down goose fat is (as my recipes occasionally reveal) often replaced by butter, even in Périgord itself, since it is no longer an everyday by-product of the Dordogne kitchen and is expensive to buy. Nevertheless, if you are roasting or cooking a goose it would be a shame not to render down the fat and try it out with some of these recipes. All the loose fat inside the fowl is pulled out and chopped into small pieces. In half a pint of water the pieces are simmered in a covered saucepan for twenty-five minutes. The pan is then uncovered and the liquid boiled slowly. This slowly evaporates the water from the fat. The fat will begin to splutter and spit. As soon as this stops, the fat is rendered. It ought to be a pale yellow in colour, with the fatty particles a light brown. Strain the liquid into a storage jar. This strained fat can be kept in a refrigerator for several weeks.

Another characteristic of this cuisine are dishes that could be cooked over an open fire. In many households these outlived the introduction of the wood-burning stove, and some people prefer them today for slowly cooked dishes. Either a pot may be hung over the fire, or a heavy-based pot placed in the ashes themselves or in the hearth. An extraordinary number of dishes would originally have been cooked like this: soups, poultry, fish stews, stuffed vegetables and even cakes. Of the soups of the Dordogne, there are two regional specialities you find everywhere: le tourain, a thin broth, and le sobronade, a solid and satisfying soup which leaves little appetite for a second course. Of the two I prefer le tourain. This I learnt to cook, curiously, through one of my cousins. He and his wife were staying in a gîte, one of the privately owned holiday homes let to tourists and usually attached to farms. They had struck

up an excellent friendship with the wife who ran the *gîte*, and we sat
in her kitchen and watched her cook this. It is the simplest of many
versions of the soup and very good.

🔥

> For this **Tourain à l'oseille** she took three or four cloves
> of garlic and some sorrel leaves and slowly cooked them
> in goose fat. To this she added a tablespoonful of flour
> and mixed in about 1½ litres of water. Adding salt and
> pepper she set this to boil for twenty minutes, during
> which time she added the white of an egg, letting it
> coagulate. In traditional Dordogne fashion she cut up
> some pieces of bread with a crust – country *tourtes* are
> preferable to *baguettes* – and put these into the soup. At
> this point we left to take a pre-prandial drink, but later I
> asked her what she had done to finish this *tourain*. She
> simply let it cool and then, away from the heat, added the
> yolk of the egg mixed with a tablespoonful of vinegar as a
> thickener.

Towards the end of your soup you can *faire chabrol* – a fine
Dordogne custom, still observed quite unselfconsciously by many
a local as he eats his soup. In a posh restaurant I do not yet dare *faire
chabrol*. But usually, out of the corner of your eye, you can see
someone unconsciously bold enough to do so. Instead of completely emptying the soup bowl, the custom is to pour into the
dregs of the soup a little red wine. The warmth of the soup releases
the flavour of the wine, which in turn enhances the flavour of the
bouillon, and the diner raises the bowl to his lips and happily drinks
it down. In the days of Jacquou le Croquant the practice was
deemed to promote all manner of physical well-being. And a patois
rhyme still sings of its health-giving properties:

> 'Qu'ei lou chabrol que ravicolo
> Qu'ei lou pu grand dous medicis.'

('It's *chabrol* which revives your strength/Which is the finest of all
medicines.')

Sobronade is traditionally regarded in Périgord as a soup but is really a mash of white beans and potatoes, flavoured with ham – a poor man's *cassoulet*.

♨

> To make **Sobronade**, take 750 grammes of white beans, 250 grammes of little square pieces of ham and 500 grammes of fat and lean pork. Cover them in cold water, boil and skim. To the casserole add three or four carrots, an onion spiked with cloves and two or three thickly sliced turnips (some of these, if possible, having already been fried in goose fat). Season, cover the casserole and boil the dish for another twenty-five minutes. Then 250 grammes of thickly sliced potatoes are added and the whole soup is cooked gently for 1½ hours. To make the *sobronade* even solider (and to use up food that might otherwise be wasted) the dish is served poured over slices of stale bread.

In the same spirit of economy, the farmers' wives are adept at making old fowl tender and full of flavour. I have seen my neighbours cutting the flesh of the bird into pieces, adding finely sliced pieces of pork, six carrots, six sliced onions and some parsley, before cooking the whole dish in a casserole. Just before cooking they pour over the fowl a large glass of cognac, another of white wine. They boil – not simmer – the dish for a quarter of an hour, add a pint of broth, cover the casserole and cook for two hours in the oven.

If you need a chicken for the evening meal, you can always buy one from the local farmers. My own preference is to ask not for a chicken but for a duck. Usually I ask not Mme Véril Henri but her sister-in-law, Mme Véril Moïse, who lives on the other side of our village, for a nice fleshy bird. To buy one like this is a privilege. Most of what these farms produce is sold on the market in Sarlat, and to kill a duck out of turn disrupts the regular pattern of country life.

As a further favour, when you buy a duck you may well be offered advice on the best way of cooking it. I buy my ducks plucked but not cleaned. 'Keep the liver and the gizzard', says Mme Véril, 'when you clean it.' This is how she told me to cook duck.

🔥

For a **Canard aux oignons** skin twenty small onions. Season the inside of the duck with salt and pepper. Rub a clove of garlic on a piece of bread. Break this up and put it inside the duck, along with the liver and the gizzard, four or five sage leaves and some leaves of thyme. Sew up the duck. Heat 150 ml of oil in a casserole and brown the duck all over. Cut 75 grammes of fresh bacon into pieces, and place at the bottom of the casserole. Place the duck on top with the onions around it. Salt and pepper, and put between the onions a sprig of thyme and a little sage. Pour over a cupful of stock. Cover the casserole and place into a medium oven for 1½ hours or until the bird is cooked. Remove the duck from the casserole and cut it up. Skim any fat from the remaining sauce, and spoon the sauce over the duck and the onions.

Restaurants tend to produce a duck that is far too dry for my taste. Pot-roasting it in this way, covered and with the added stock, keeps the flesh deliciously moist.

The housewives also have their own ways with fish. One dish I have never seen in Dordogne hotels is a *matelote*, or stew of river fish and eels, cooked with red wine but without the customary addition of mushrooms or cognac. Although the fish – be it carp or perch – is skinned, usually the skin of the eel is thrown in with the rest, a practice that to my taste makes the dish far too fatty. However, this is how they cook it.

🔥

For an unadorned **Matelote** scale and clean a carp or perch. Cut off its head. Cut this fish and the eels into large pieces and roll them in flour. Place in a cauldron about twenty-five small skinned onions and, stirring all the time, add a heaped dessertspoonful of flour. To this sauce add 600 ml of fairly strong red wine – it is important to help reduce the oiliness – salt and pepper, bay leaves, parsley, a bunch of thyme and a clove of garlic. When the onions are half cooked, add the pieces of fish and simmer for twenty minutes. (If you wish, add the skin of the eel now, too.) Before the dish is served, take out the bunch of thyme.

I prefer this straightforward *matelote* to one enriched with a butter *roux*.

Chou farci is a delicacy known throughout France (and in other lands too), a classic way of giving flavour and variety to a vegetable once eaten daily. Each place cherishes its own way of preparing the dish. The stuffing made by my neighbours is not especially distinctive – minced veal, fat bacon, garlic, onion, tarragon, parsley, breadcrumbs and eggs – but the short cooking time is unusual. After stuffing, the cabbage is cooked only *à point*, for no more than a quarter of an hour in water or, preferably, *bouillon* to which has been added a glass of white wine. This avoids the soggy football effect sometimes found. I have always eaten it hot, but elsewhere in the *département* I believe it is sometimes served cold.

The delicious local turnips, by contrast, are more often stuffed with a pork forcemeat.

For **Navets farcis**, always buy good quality sausage-meat. Boil the turnips whole for five minutes in salted water. Slice off the lids and hollow them out. Mince the pulp with seasoned pork sausagemeat. Fill the turnips with this mixture, put back the lids and set them in a baking dish. Sprinkle with breadcrumbs and a little melted butter, and brown them in the oven.

A far more unusual dish, in my mind almost magically associated with this region on the principle made famous by Proust's *madeleines*, is a cake of maize and wheat flour known in the local patois as a *rimote* or *milassou*. I first came across *rimote* in the Vézère Valley, I am almost certain at Montignac. I had never come across anything like it before and the word was not in my pocket dictionary. It seemed to have a magical taste. Later, I found out that it is one of a number of pancakes, dumplings, cakes and biscuits made with the cornmeal that largely replaced millet as a staple after the introduction of maize from the New World. Another is *millias*, a pumpkin and cornmeal cake with rum and brandy. This simpler version, also known as *pous*, is boiled then fried rather than baked.

&

Rimote is an amazingly simple dish, cooked out of 125 grammes of maize flour, 100 grammes of goose fat, an egg, two soupspoonfuls of wheat flour and some cheese (usually Gruyère) – 100 grammes or so. Boil in a stewpot 500 ml of salted water, pour in the maize flour and stir it with a wooden spatula until you have a thick porridge. Add two soupspoonfuls of the goose fat, mix well and take off the heat. Lightly grease your work- surface, spread out the porridge over it to a thickness of about three millimetres, smooth it out and let it cool. Beat the egg. Sprinkle the wheat flour over part of your work surface. With a sharp knife, cut squares from the porridge mixture, brush them with the egg and pass them through the wheat flour. Golden both sides in a frying pan in the remainder of the goose fat. Serve immediately, sprinkled with grated Gruyère. A sweet biscuit, *cruchade*, is made in the same way, but eaten sprinkled with lemon and sugar.

For me, however, the taste of *rimotes*, remains magical. I think of it always as I drive past the racks of dried maize, or corn cobs, my neighbours use to feed their cows.

Although dishes like *sobronade*, *chou farci* and *rimote* are made all the year round, they are exceptional. Most everyday dishes are seasonal, not from human whim but from necessity, from the ingredients available before the age of the refrigerator or imported hothouse fruit and vegetables. The need to cope with recurring months of scarcity always stimulates the art of making preserves, and they are now regarded as a speciality of the region. In the summer months *mirabelle* plums, melons, apricots and cherries are made into jams or bottled. In the winter months, farmers' wives will be making the famous *confits* of Périgord – pork, duck and geese cooked and sealed in airtight jars. Preserved goose (*confit d'oie*) is the speciality of our region. Great jars of it are seen in all the shops of Domme. This is how Adrienne Desplat makes it.

🕯️

Cut the goose for the **Confit d'oie** into joints and remove all the fat from the inside. Rub the joints all over thoroughly with sea salt and place them in an earthenware dish. Leave to stand for six days. Melt down the goose fat. At the end of six days wash the goose and place it in an ovenproof dish. Cover the joints with the fat and cook in a moderate oven for three hours (or until the goose is cooked). Pack the joints into suitable containers. Allow the liquid fat to cool down and then pour over the goose so that it is absolutely covered. Cover the container with foil, and then use as required.

In Adrienne's extensive kitchen row after row of these preserves are stacked in their stoneware jars.

🕯️

The method for **Confit de canard** is different: the meat is simmered off the bone. The flesh of the duck is taken from its legs, wings and shoulders and cut into pieces. Surplus fat is cut off before the rest is covered in coarse salt, and left for forty-eight hours. Surplus salt is then washed away and the pieces boiled, turning frequently, not allowing them to boil too violently until, when pricked with a fork, golden – and not pink – juice is emitted. Put the pieces in jars, sealed with grease, until you need to eat them.

Confits may simply be eaten as it is with bread, or grilled, used in casseroles and stuffings. There are endless variations to these *confits*. In Sarlat potatoes are added, elsewhere pork and goose is mixed. Certainly the flavour is improved by preserving in fat rather than a sterilised, vacuum-sealed jar.

For the Dordogne farmer the winter is a placid season. My

neighbours have little to do outside the house. They clip the vines where necessary. They prune their trees, taking special care of young walnut trees. They look ahead and chop firewood for their stoves, fires and, today, central heating. The evenings are extremely pleasant during these winter months. Until March people shell walnuts, sometimes inviting friends to join them, drinking a little of the *vin nouveau* that they made the previous October, telling stories and reminiscing about the past. Sometimes they add a little alcoholic spice to an evening by taking a glass of liqueur.

By mid-February the ground is warming up. The rain continues to fall. In the country, all eyes are very finely tuned to the effects of the rain, especially its ability to bring out new sources of nourishment. Snails known as *cagouilles* come out of their hiding places. These are assiduously collected throughout Périgord. They are a form of *escargot*, though juicier and often slightly larger.

&

With or without their shells, **Cagouilles** are cooked in *bouillon*. If you do not shell them, add garlic, fat, endives, salt and pepper to the *bouillon*, as well as a glass of white wine. Cooked this way *cagouilles* are eaten with mayonnaise. Cooked out of their shells, *cagouilles* are usually eaten with a sauce like a *béchamel* from onions sautéed in either olive or walnut oil, flour and milk, garnished with garlic, parlsey and goose fat.

This is the time to prepare seedling beds for tobacco plants, a task that may take till mid-March. The work is now increasing. It is time in March to start manuring fields and planting barley and wheat. With Easter arrives spring and much more work. In April you see the farmers and their families planting maize. Now, too, is the time to start spraying the vines with sulphate and copper oxide diluted in water. By May vegetation is growing apace in this fertile land.

Even some of those delicious Dordogne mushrooms known as *cèpes* appear, though mostly they wait till September before leaping abundantly from wet ground. It is good to enjoy some of these early ones very simply cooked, by themselves.

&

For **Cèpes sautés** take the stalks from 350 grammes of *cèpes* and chop up the caps. Melt in a frying pan two tablespoonfuls of butter and one tablespoon of olive oil. Sauté the *cèpes* until light brown, seasoning with salt and pepper. Add, while stirring, the stalks of the *cèpes*, well chopped, as well as three peeled and chopped shallots. Toss and cook for two or three minutes. Serve sprinkled with lemon juice.

The pace of work continues to quicken. Some farmers have hardly finished planting their maize by the middle of May when it is time to transplant the tobacco seedlings into the open ground. To cap all this, the hay is ready for cutting and transforming into silage. Haymaking can continue into June and July, and these are also the months to start picking and preserving fruit. Watermelon jam, a local speciality, is made with watermelon, simmered with ginger, cinnamon and sugar for eight hours. If there is any spare time, the farmer is busy fixing fences and generally keeping his property in order. Until we bought our own equipment I used to try to find a farmer with spare time to cut the grass in our meadow. 'In principle there's no problem,' he would invariably reply, 'but I'll have to wait till I find time to cut it.' Our grass grew. Our meadow was an unsightly mess. The farmers rarely came. Now I know what they have to do for themselves during this season, I understand why.

August brings no respite. Now the barley and wheat is ready for harvesting. It is time, too, to start searching out winter firewood. And scarcely is this done when the grapes must be gathered from the vines, so that wine-making, which takes place between mid-September and mid-October, can begin. Although only the western parts of Périgord grow wines for serious trading and export, some 35,000 proprietors cultivate vines for selling to the general public. Their *vin ordinaire* is by no means rubbish. Something like 50% of the harvest is carried out these days by machines. Modern technology is taking some of the uncertainty out of wine-making, enabling the *vignerons* to control the temperatures at which the juices ferment, to spot what might be going wrong by means of more rigorously scientific tests than the old peasant farmer employed.

But to make wines is still a traditional skill; and élsewhere in the Dordogne traditional methods still prevail. Each farmer, however small his property, has parcels of land set aside for producing his own wine and nearly everyone else grows at least a few vines, often trained across a trellis to give shade as well as grapes. The many times I have watched my neighbours pruning their vines has left me still ignorant of the mysteries of this essential work. Vines need manure – but, warns my neighbour Michel, 'not too much'. Only his own innate skills tell him exactly what 'too much' amounts to. He also keeps an anxious eye for any sort of mouldiness on his trees.

To be offered some home-made wine is a great privilege. You can taste the freshness, and the sweetness of the grapes from these tiny vineyards – *vin ordinaire* no doubt, but very pure, with no chemical nonsense in the bottle.

Throughout all this time the tobacco crop has never been far from the minds of these farmers. In spite of modern methods, growing tobacco is still time-consuming and occasionally back-breaking. Today it is no longer sown by hand, but planted by machine – drawn along by a tractor, the womenfolk sitting on the machine itself, dropping the seeds to be sown every fourteen inches or so. After the seeds have been transplanted in May, weeding, hoeing and earthing up the plants keeps whole farming families busy. Although latterly stronger disease-resistant strains of tobacco have been introduced to the Dordogne from America, the crops need to be sprayed against harmful insects. And once flowers start to appear, they need to be speedily removed to encourage more leaves to grow.

Even today old-fashioned ways of curing tobacco vie with newer methods. The tobacco is cut from mid-August to mid-September, provided the plant is not too dry (when work must stop). It is loaded on carts and carried to great barns, with tiled roofs and shutters to regulate the passage of air and the humidity. Hung upside down, the tobacco is dried, before being divided for processing. The upper leaves, the middle leaves and the base are processed separately. The more modern process, for *tabac blond*, involves drying the plants in large ovens and takes only five or six days. The plants are then made into bales of thirty kilogrammes and sent to be made into cigarettes. The 4,500 tobacco farmers of Périgord all belong to the Service d'Exploitation Industrielle des

Tabacs et Allumettes – SEITA for short – and from November to March regularly deliver the different parts of the plant to local depots.

By the time the tobacco harvest is finished, the pace of work is at last slowing down. There is time to put on wellingtons and search in the woods for the *cèpes* that suddenly appear when the weather is sufficiently humid in September. Dishes using *cèpes* may always be made with field mushrooms. *Cèpes* cooked in the old Dordogne way are neither washed nor peeled but cleaned with a damp piece of linen. If possible, too, use an earthenware dish to cook them in.

For these **Cèpes à la vieille mode périgourdine**, cut the stalks off the *cèpes*. On a hot flame warm good olive oil. Put in the *cèpes* very gently, so as not to bruise them. Gently sauté them, turning frequently and being careful not to dry them. Reduce the heat and add parsley and finely chopped garlic. Serve them on a hot plate, sprinkle on lemon juice and eat them with wooden cutlery.

The ways in which the people of Périgord use these *cèpes* in cooking seem to me endless. With a stuffing made of minced ham and bacon, breadcrumbs mashed in milk, finely chopped parsley and garlic, salt, pepper, and eggs for binding, the heads of large, open *cèpes* are placed one on top of the other in a casserole and very slowly cooked in fat, with a little bouillon added from time to time so that the dish does not become too dry, for delicious *cèpes farcis*. *Oronges* are frequently washed, their stalks removed, lightly dipped in oil and then grilled for three or four minutes – quite gently so as not to crisp them too much; *rosés des prés* are often substituted for *cèpes* in omelettes; sliced *mousserons* give flavour to the sauces that accompany many a roast meat. They are also served sautéed in oil or fat. Salt and pepper them, cover the pan and let them cook for a quarter of an hour. Then reduce, before adding some finely chopped parsley and shallots, and perhaps a hint of unfermented grape juice or lemon juice.

September is also the month for killing the geese. The goose farm near us takes on a company of women who pluck, clean and cut up the geese. When they have finished, not a morsel remains on their work-benches. The feathers are saved for pillows and duvets. Even the feet of a goose eventually make glue or some other synthetic product. Of the rest is created all manner of delicious dishes. As usual nothing goes to waste. One of my old friends, a widow that I meet in Grolejac church on Sundays, once told me how she loves to eat the anus of a goose, 'crisply fried' as she put it. I would not go that far. But here are a few unusual dishes that evolved before the days when *abatis* – giblets, wing tips and gizzards – were considered fit only for making stock. They are surprisingly good and worth trying if you have bought another whole bird, such as a turkey, capon or duck.

The September *cèpes* and chestnuts enhance goose and duck giblets.

♣

To make **Gésiers d'oie à la mode périgourdine**, cut 450 grammes of giblets into pieces and fry for fifteen minutes in two tablespoonfuls of goose fat. Transfer to a large casserole. Blanche 225 grammes of salsifies and fry this, too, in the goose fat. Parboil 450 grammes of carrots. Fry six *cèpes* in the fat, and add them to the casserole, along with a little *bouillon*. Add twelve roasted chestnuts, the carrots, *bouquet garni*, salt and pepper, and cook for three to four hours over a low heat.

The very tips of a goose's wings are used to make a traditional *ragoût* called *alicot*, from the patois for *ailes cuites* (cooked wings).

♣

Alicot is made in a saucepan. Warm goose fat and lightly brown the tips of the wings. Take them out. Add sliced carrots, shallots, onions, chopped garlic. Take them out. Make a *roux* with the fat and flour and thin with stock or wine. Put back the wings, make sure there is enough liquid to cover them and cook for about ninety minutes.

The old way with gizzards in the country farms of Périgord is to scrape out the interior flesh. This is lightly salted and left to stand for a couple of days, then grilled and conserved in goose fat. It is eaten warmed through in a *bouillon* with chopped vegetables and a *bouquet garni*. Sometimes the farmer's wife throws pieces of potato and some tomatoes into the *ragoût* as well.

A fourth traditional Dordogne method of cooking a goose is *aux marrons*, a subtler dish than the other three, perhaps:

The chestnuts in **Oie brasée aux marrons** are cooked in stock until more than half done. Then these are minced with pork forcemeats and used to stuff the goose, which is tied up, roasted and served in its own sauce.

By October, when there can be a nip in the air, hunting has begun in earnest. Every week-end the forests are peopled by men with dogs and guns. They dress in green, wearing forage caps. Some act as beaters, attempting to drive the animals to where other men wait in long rows. The people of Périgord keep two separate attitudes to the lovely animals of the forests. They are exquisite and have to be protected. In season they also make an extremely succulent dish. In the end it is obviously in the interests of the hunters that these precious animals should not be pursued to destruction and total extinction. Nevertheless, the temptation is continually to kill more animals than the rigorous law allows. The prestigious Fédération Départementale of the huntsmen of the Dordogne tries to keep its members in order, pursuing delinquents and urging them to restrain their greed, if only in the interests of preserving enough animals for the supply not to run out. But in spite of numerous annual prosecutions of offenders, it is unlikely that self-discipline prevents huntsmen bagging more than their fair share of game. As well as the large animals, such as wild boar, whose survival makes the Fédération particularly important as a force for conservation, smaller game, such as deer and hind, are now at risk.

I never cease to marvel at the dedication to hunting. Every week-end the menfolk line the long winding road to our village, double-barrelled guns at the ready, cigarettes hanging glumly from their lips, dogs prowling around – and never a deer in sight. One of our friends and his wife owns a local hotel and restaurant. Each

Saturday during the season, whatever the weather, he abandons all the work to her and goes to stand with his friends by the roadside, in the apparently regulation melancholy fashion, usually returning empty-handed. His wife tells us she always cooks him rabbit, since rabbit is all he has ever managed to shoot.

I was once taught two traditional ways for killing rabbits by a woman from Grolejac. For some time after this conversation I noticed that none of us was choosing rabbit dishes whenever we went out to eat and I must confess that I do not think I shall ever make use of this advice. However, the information is interesting and may have its uses for the less squeamish. The first method is to introduce a funnel into the rabbit's mouth. Place the animal between your legs, its head in the air and its body stretched out, holding it by the ears. Then pour into the funnel the contents of a glass of *eau-de-vie*. This poisons the rabbit without poisoning the person who will later eat it.

You use the second method when you need to keep the rabbit's blood. Stun the animal by hitting it on the base of its neck. Then with a pocket knife either cut its carotid (one of the two arteries in the neck) or skewer out one eye. Holding it upside down by its legs, you can then easily pour the blood into a bowl.

❦

The rabbit is usually made into **Lapereau en casserole**. It is cut into pieces and added to 125 grammes of *lardons* or bacon, cut into cubes, and cooked gently in heated fat for twenty minutes. When it is well browned, a chopped shallot, 80 grammes of celeriac cut into small pieces, two bay leaves, three sprigs of parsley and a pinch of thyme are added. The mixture is salted and peppered. Half a glass of white wine is mixed with half a glass of stock and poured over the rabbit. The dish is cooked gently for ten minutes, care being taken that it does not boil. Then the casserole is covered and cooked – again very gently – for half an hour, stirring from time to time.

There are endless variations to this method. A good red wine casserole may be made with small onions, garlic and *cèpes* for flavouring.

I often ask myself whether the British have some inherent dislike of eating hare. Many of our visitors seem to steer clear of it whenever we take them to our local restaurants and they do not always seem to relish my wife buying a hare from the butcher. I wonder if there is not still some faint suspicion that this is wartime fare, somehow second-best, to be discarded when the good times returned? The French have no such lingering nonsense clogging up their gastronomic psyche. In the patois of the Dordogne they call the hare '*uno penudo*' – that is, one that runs on bare feet. They love to hunt such a worthy opponent. The Périgord is known for a classic dish from its chateaux, *lièvre à la royale*. But the Dordogne housewife cooks her hare with equal subtlety and much less pretentiousness. Here is one of her methods:

🕯️

For **Lièvre à la campagne** take a hare weighing two kilos and clean it. Put the heart and the liver into a bowl, with the animal's blood. Add two soupspoonfuls of vinegar to the liver, heart and blood, and mix together. Cover and put in the fridge or a cool place. Put the hare into a terrine. Add chopped carrots and onions, two crushed cloves of garlic, a little thyme, parsley, bay leaf, salt and pepper. Soak overnight in red wine and oil. The next day take out the hare, and with a fine knife remove the fine bones on either side of its breastbone and ribs. Prepare a stuffing with 250 grammes of minced fillet of pork, 250 grammes of bacon (reserving the fat), two spring onions, half the heart and liver of the hare and fine herbs, seasoned and bound with one egg. Cut into small pieces 250 grammes of veal. Stuff the hare methodically, first with a quarter of the bacon fat, then half the veal, then more bacon fat and then all the prepared stuffing; repeat with more bacon fat, the rest of the veal and finally a last layer of the bacon fat. Every part of the hare's inside should be filled, stuffed in this way. Sew up the hole. Wrap some more bacon fat around the hare, tying it with string. Sauté the hare in goose fat over a hot flame until the surface is browned. Then place it in a large casserole with any of the bacon that is left, as well as the carrots and onions from the marinade. Pour over the liquid from the marinade and, if you wish, two teaspoonfuls of Armagnac and cook gently for half an hour. Then pour over one cupful of veal stock. Cover the casserole, and place in a medium oven to cook very slowly for four hours. Fifteen minutes before the hare is cooked, blend or mash with a fork the blood, the remaining heart and liver, along with two cloves of garlic. Pour this sauce into a pan, and simmer gently for ten minutes. Carefully take the hare out of the casserole; remove the string. Mix the juices from the casserole with the sauce, and pour this over the hare ready for serving.

Throughout the months of October and November game-birds are also hunted. To bag a pheasant is particularly praiseworthy. Plucked and cleaned, the bird is often casseroled in a manner reminiscent of Normandy until one remembers that in November the farmers are gathering in their apples here.

☋

In a **Faisan en cocotte** the farmers' wives often place slices of dessert apples on the bottom of the casserole before placing the pheasant (already browned in fat on both sides) on top, surrounded by more slices of apple. Cream is poured over the bird, and perhaps some *eau-de-vie* or cognac. The casserole is covered and the whole cooked for another half-hour or so in a moderate oven.

The more humble pigeon is equally delicious provided you take care not to swallow any pellets of shot that the hunter might have left inside. Sometimes they do not appear on menus and the huntsmen fail to bag any because it is a cold autumn. One year I was told that the wild ones, *palombes*, had unfortunately flown to the Lot because of a sudden, unusually severe nip in the air. But once you have caught your game bird, the ways of serving it are mouth-watering.

☋

It is often prepared as **Palombe à la crapaudine**. Choose four tender pigeons. Truss these birds, securing their legs and wings with string. Place them on a dish and brush with a little oil and butter. Make a stuffing by mixing together the pigeon's livers, some smoked bacon which has been boiled in water, drained and chopped, *bouquet garni*, a little minced veal, the yolk of an egg and, if it is available, a little finely flaked *truffe*. Mix thoroughly. Stuff the pigeons, put strips of fat over the birds and place them in a roasting tin. Roast in a medium heat. When cooked, place on a serving dish, pouring over them the juice of two lemons.

I could here describe other recipes for small game birds, but I will not. Sometimes when I am working at my desk on a very mild autumn day, with the door and windows to the south side of the house open, a delightful thing happens. Attracted, I think, by the clatter of my typewriter, a couple of swallows fly in through the door. They perch, virtually upside-down, on the old beams. I think, though I'm not certain, that they are busy gobbling tiny insects in the wood. They do not seem to mind at all if I walk around seeking inspiration. Occasionally they fly out through the south windows and, in a trice, swoop in again through the open north door. Although they are legally protected, swallows are not immune from the huntsmen. Sitting in my home there while the birds swoop in and out, I must say I could never bring myself to eat a swallow, however well cooked.

The Rhythm of Life:
Continuity and Change

'There is no history of cuisine that is not also a
history of prevailing appetite, habits and taste.'

JEAN-CLAUDE REVEL

The rhythm of life in the Dordogne is not only that of the seasons,
but also that of the church year. The often exquisite old churches
scattered everywhere in the *département* are also a reminder of the
importance of faith in earlier centuries. No visitor to the Dordogne
today should miss seeing the remarkable church of St Front, in
Périgueux, still scarcely known outside this *département* and far less
celebrated than Sacré Coeur de Montmartre in Paris, which, in fact,
it inspired. This fantastic building was reconstructed in the tenth
and eleventh centuries as a western counterpart – though no mere
copy – of the church of the Holy Apostles in Constantinople, much
pillaged and neglected and then superbly restored in the late
nineteenth century. Several towns of the region – Bergerac, for
example – were also resting places for pilgrims on their way to
venerate the relics of St James at Santiago de Compostela in Spain.
That many British made this pilgrimage is unconsciously commemorated in a curious street-name at Bergerac: the pilgrim church
there stands on the corner of the Rue St Jacques and the Rue St
Jâmes. Today, the churches and shrines are often empty. Many
abbeys have become museums, markets or town halls. One such
shrine, the superb and yet gentle flamboyant Gothic monastery at
Cadouin – now the property of the state – thankfully remains intact.

Inside the monastery church the pillars of the apse retain their medieval colours; the fresco of the Resurrection still moves the pilgrim. Candles burn before a late-sixteenth-century statue of the Virgin Mary. But the Holy Shroud of Cadouin, which men once claimed had wrapped the head of the dead Christ, was in 1934 proved to be an eleventh-century fake. The shroud is no longer displayed in Cadouin church but – rightly, I hold – no-one has been boorish enough to take down the twenty-three plaques thanking the shroud for bestowing blessings on those who in the past revered it as genuine. Belief has declined dramatically and continues to do so, at least as it is observed outwardly. Ordinands began declining by 200 a year in the 1970s and throughout France today fewer than a hundred men each year are ordained! Scarcely one priest in ten is aged under forty. Although 79% of the French population claims to be Catholic, only 12% regularly attend Mass on Sundays. Services are being cut down and parishes amalgamated.

No services at all take place in the little church that supports the yellow post-box at the end of our village. I worship in Grolejac, where the romanesque church has an exquisite apse with beautifully cleaned stones, and is covered with a roof of ancient stones (known locally as *lauzes*). Yet even there few attend – though tourists swell our congregations – and now the priest, who lives in Carsac and cares for several other churches too, comes only once a fortnight.

Occasionally our own little church is full: once, over forty persons arrived for a baptism. During the service everyone in the congregation was handed a piece of dry, sweet baptism-cake, which was blessed with holy water before we ate it. Afterwards we were all invited into the gardens of the château that stands next to the church, whether we knew the baby's family or not. There we drank champagne and ate more of the baptism-cake. But alas the priest could not join us; indicatively he had to speed away to celebrate another mass elsewhere.

Marriages are still sometimes celebrated in church. The customs attached to it die hard. On some evenings I can still persuade my Dordogne neighbours to speak of *charivaris* – vehicles for ridiculing those who had made some incautious step towards marriage – say, a notorious adulterer, an old lady marrying a young man, or a widower taking a new wife before his old one had been long enough in the grave. These seem to have been vicious. Disorderly behaviour outside the homes of the supposed offenders, mocking songs, raucous assembling, the banging of pots and pans, must have proved embarrasingly offensive to the victims of the *charivari*. In the Dordogne if such a victim did not pay a few *sous* to his or her tormentors, the children might keep up their antics for over a fortnight. Death is observed too. One of the most curious monuments in this region is the bizarre Lanterne des Morts, built to commemorate a visit to Sarlat by St Bernard in 1147. No-one could squeeze a fully grown dead body into the Lanterne. Almost certainly lights would have been burned inside this curious edifice when the body of some noted citizen lay in state inside the cathedral. Today, on All Souls' Day, the graveyards are still blessed and prayers offered for the souls of those whose bodies lie there. In preparation for the priest's visit, our villagers (like countless others) clip the hedge of our little cemetery, renew the plastic flowers, dig over the graves and straighten up fallen stones with their sad inscriptions (*'Ici repose un ange'* etc.). The work is much needed, since graveyards are miserably neglected for most of the year in our part of France.

In the past these religious feast days were far more than holy days – they set the rhythms of country life as much as the seasons of the years did. To take just one example, a hundred years ago laundry was only done on set feast days: at the New Year, in Holy Week, on All Souls' Day and on Rogation Day. To launder meant to soak and boil precious and rare linen, and most peasant families possessed but one – to cover as many people as possible, in one bed.

But if the religious feast days are no longer celebrated by full churches, they are a rarely missed opportunity for family gatherings, and for traditional dishes cooked as they have been for centuries – although they are eaten alongside other far more lavish dishes than peasant families could have afforded in the past.

Many people barely glimpse this part of life in Périgord because they are only able to visit in summer, rather than the quieter seasons. For this reason, I feel an immense sense of privilege to share in life there as Christmas approaches. The streets of the towns and villages are decorated – these days with electric light-bulbs, but never garishly. The 'Traverse' in Sarlat, for example, is lit with differently coloured bulbs and numerous stars of Bethlehem, and in the winding medieval streets softer lights play on many of the ancient buildings. The oil-sheikh who now owns and has carefully restored château Montfort (and is known locally as the Emir) gives the whole neighbourhood a treat by illuminating Montfort at night. In our own village only the red berries of cotoneaster are adding colour to the ochre stones of the village, matching the breast of the robin who comes here every year. These days he refuses to leave the handle of my spade until I actually pick it up.

From the supermarket or the nurseryman on Sarlat market we buy a Christmas tree with roots, in the hope that it will transplant to the meadow on twelfth night. The idea was inspired by a Dutchman whose home is only a few kilometres from our house and who has perhaps twenty such trees, each one a year's growth taller than the next, reminders of the past and also that Christmas is a symbol of birth and the promise of new life. The first time we tried we failed miserably. The tree took root in the ground without any problem. February was a rainy month, which helped it to establish itself. Then the drought came. The meadow turned yellow. M. Véril worried about the vines. We watered our plants and young trees as much as we could. I thought that we might just save the Christmas tree. Then it died, quickly, in one day. In the morning the top part and one side was browny-yellow and brittle. The following morning not a single branch was alive. I dug it up and we put it on the fire.

At *réveillon* – both the eve of Christmas and the eve of the New Year – traditionally the people here would eat black puddings and drink a hot spiced wine. Some of them still do, resisting the artificial rituals of the intrusive television.

The plump turkeys once confined to the great houses of noble families fill the market stalls and are one of the traditional Christmas dishes, stuffed with truffles. They are usually prepared the day before cooking so that the flesh of the bird becomes imbued with the scent of the truffles.

&

To cook **Dinde truffée** for six people, you need a young bird weighing around three kilos, 200 grammes of ham, two *foies* from other fowl, five truffles, two shallots, 100 grammes of breadcrumbs, milk, salt and pepper, two eggs, 75 grammes of goose fat and a soupspoonful of cognac. Clean and pluck the turkey (if you cannot persuade the butcher or farmer to do this for you) and keep its liver. Slice one of the truffles and gently insert it under the flesh around the bird's collar. Make the stuffing by mincing the turkey's liver and the two extra ones, along with the ham, the shallots and the parsley; add the breadcrumbs and the milk, working in the eggs. Add pepper but not salt. Work in the skins of the remaining truffles, the cognac and any truffle juice. Mix this stuffing with the remaining truffles, which should be left whole. Now stuff the turkey. Close it up and leave overnight. Cook it in a hot oven, basting with the goose fat. Cooking will take between two and three hours. Make sure that the bird does not become dry. The cooking is finished when the juice of the turkey is white.

These days even the fairly well-to-do often dispense with the expensive truffles, replacing them with chestnuts. We prefer a succulent farm-reared duck or goose to turkey, and then follow a very fine Dordogne recipe, with a chestnut stuffing. It could equally well be used for turkey, and is absolutely delicious.

❧

For a **Oie aux marrons**, start by making the stuffing. Place in a saucepan 750 grammes of fresh chestnuts, two stalks of celery, a *bouquet garni* and 650 ml of stock. Simmer gently for an hour. Drain, leave to cool, and peel them, as for *châtaignes blanchies*, page 113. Gently cook 1.8 kilos of very finely chopped onions until they are tender. Put them into a large bowl. Pour 125 ml of Madeira into the frying pan and boil to reduce it by half. Pour this into the mixing bowl. Add to it 380 grammes of lean pork and 380 grammes of lean minced veal, two lightly beaten eggs, one teaspoonful of salt, a pinch of pepper, thyme and one clove of garlic. Mix all the ingredients together. Chop and sauté the goose liver in butter. Add the sautéed liver to the stuffing. Season the cavity of the goose with salt. Stuff the cavity with alternate layers of chestnuts and stuffing, leaving a space at the end. Sew up the goose and prick its skin. Dry the flesh thoroughly and place it, breast upwards, on a roasting tin. Roast at very high heat for about twenty minutes until the skin is brown, and then cook at 325°F. Heat some goose fat in a frying pan and some add sliced onions and carrots. Stir in 50 grammes of flour and brown slowly. Remove the pan and add 750 ml of stock and 625 ml of dry white wine. Simmer. Pour this sauce around the goose. Cover and place in the middle of the oven at 325°F. Braise for about 2½ hours. When the goose is done, the juices run pale yellow. Remove the goose to a serving dish. Skim off the fat and boil the sauce until quite thick. Stir in a wine glass of port and simmer for two minutes. Strain the sauce through a sieve into a bowl. Pour some over the goose and serve. This is a very rich dish, and you will probably need a respite before moving on to the next course.

Of course I bring from Britain plum pudding and mince pies, so as not to miss the British Christmas delights, which are also highly rated by the French we have discovered. Both mince-meat and *le cake*, fruit cake, are held in considerable esteem. Every French family finishes the meal with a *bûche de Noël* – literally a Yule log, with chestnuts. You can buy them everywhere. You can also make your own.

🕯️

This is how a **Bûche aux châtaignes** is made: Take 80 grammes of sugar, 80 grammes of flour, 20 grammes of butter, three eggs plus one yolk. Beat the yolks of the eggs and the sugar in a bowl until they are light coloured. Sprinkle in the flour. Beat the egg whites until they are stiff, and gently fold in the mixture, adding also the melted butter. Line a baking tin with buttered greaseproof paper. Pour the mixture evenly into the baking tin and bake in a pre-heated moderate oven for eight to ten minutes. Turn out the cake on to a piece of marble with paper on top. Take the greaseproof paper off the cake and cover the cake in a napkin to keep it moist and soft. Boil 225 grammes of skinned chestnuts in milk, with sugar and vanilla essence. Purée with a blender, food processor or sieve and add 100 grammes of butter, two yolks and 100 grammes of chocolate which has been melted in a little water. Adjust the consistency if necessary with icing sugar or butter. Spread three-quarters of the cream on to the cake and roll it into the shape of a log. Cover and decorate with the remaining cream, plus 50 grammes of melted chocolate or butter cream. Pattern it with a fork. To give the *bûche* a snowy effect use chantilly cream and holly leaves.

New Year's Eve, the feast of St Silvester, is a time for communal rather than family feasting. Today groups of villagers – up to two dozen at a table – arrange to eat together in local hotels, starting late, say about eleven o'clock in the evening, eating oysters and smoked salmon, sometimes dancing in long lines. When the clock strikes twelve, they still welcome the New Year in the patois of Langue d'Oc: '*Au gui lo nei*'. Not too long ago young people would make masks and prowl round the villages to delight their elders. The more grotesque the mask, the better. Some would smear their faces with honey and stick feathers all over it. All would go from door to door crying '*Au gui lo nei*', to be rewarded with a boiled egg, a coin or a cake. Now they are more likely to spend the evening dancing in discotheques to English and American pop records. Even at Christmas a Sarlat discotheque which opened its doors at 1 p.m. was packed. Order was kept by a bouncer reputed to belong to the French national judo team. I was glad not to be there.

Six days later, the feast of the Epiphany, traditionally regarded as the day when three Magi visited the infant Jesus, offers the chance to lighten the winter with another fine meal. In the Dordogne it is celebrated with *beignets*, fritters rich in eggs and sugar.

To make **Beignets soufflés** you will need 250 grammes of flour, 100 grammes of butter, one soupspoonful of sugar, a pinch of salt, 500 ml of water and eight eggs. Put boiling water into a casserole, along with the butter, cut in pieces, the sugar and the salt. Remove from the heat immediately and pour in the flour. Mix it well with a wooden spoon. Put the mixture back on the heat, continuing to stir, especially on the base and sides of the casserole. The mixture is cooked perfectly when it sticks neither to the sides of the casserole nor to the wooden spoon. Allow the paste to cool slightly. Whisk the eggs with a fork and gradually beat them into the paste. It should become glossy. Fry the *beignets* in 750 ml of oil at medium temperature, increasing the heat when you put in each batch of five or six spoonfuls of the mixture, each the size of a small egg. The fritters will start to expand, split and brown without having been touched. Remove them when they are brown, drain in a sieve and then put them on a plate, sprinkling with icing sugar. Serve them either as they are or with custard or jam.

The next major feast is Shrove Tuesday, the last day before Lent, traditionally in Périgord the day for the annual slaughtering of the pig. Sausages, *boudins*, all manner of pork dishes and *pâtés* are cooked, and one still hears the traditional patois saying of the region, '*Por cornabal, se majo de car*' – for carnival one eats meat. This was the time when *bougras*, black-pudding-water soup, was particularly relished. It is still an excellent Périgord soup, and a very good way of using the deliciously enriched water in which you have poached your *boudin*.

For **Bougras** the black puddings are poached, taken out of the water and the water brought to the boil. Measure out 2½ litres and chop up as many carrots, turnips, leeks, onions and celery as the stock will accommodate alongside a head of curly green cabbage that has been cut into pieces and blanched. The mixture is gently simmered for forty minutes, before 400 grammes of thickly sliced potatoes are added. This is cooked for another half hour. Before the dish is served two typically Dordogne touches are made. First, some of the vegetables are removed from the soup, sliced and fried in goose fat, with a sprinkling of flour and a little stock, before being added once again to the *bougras*. Secondly, the soup bowl is lined with slices of bread before the *bougras* is poured in and served.

More popular, and eaten everywhere throughout Périgord on Shrove Tuesday, are waffles – *gaufres épaisses*. These are not the hot, sticky waffles often served from open stalls on Saturday mornings at Sarlat market – or even, these days, outside some of the more popular supermarkets. Rather, they are dry, curled, and very appetising.

🕯

To make **Gaufres épaisses** you need 450 grammes of flour, six eggs, 200 grammes of sugar, three soupspoonfuls of oil, a spoonful of rum, a pinch of salt and 10 grammes of yeast mixed in a little warm milk. Put the flour on to a baking board. Make a hole and pour into it the eggs, sugar, oil, rum, salt, yeast and enough milk to make a paste which is not so thick as that for bread. Leave for a few hours. Take half a ladle of the mixture and put it into a very warm greased French waffle-iron. Quickly cook on a hot flame. As you take out the waffle, roll it around a smooth stick or the handle of a wooden spoon. Keep these waffles in an air-tight container, to preserve their crustiness.

Soon it will be Easter. To my knowledge there is no special delicacy eaten the week before, on Palm Sunday. Then, however, the church is full. Everyone cuts a twig, preferably a laurel – though this is by no means necessary – and carries it throughout the service as a reminder of the welcome of Palms given to Jesus when he rode into Jerusalem on an ass. The holy water is sprinkled over our twigs, and we carry them home. For Easter day itself there is a special bread – *le pain de Pâques*, known in the patois as *le coucou d'lo dit* (*le coq du Lot*). Bread – through the symbolic wholesomeness of wheat and because the church deployed it as a means of eternal life – was almost sacred among the poor, even though the bread they ate was always poor, frequently bad and invariably stale.

🕯

The ingredients of **Le coucou d'lo dit** are one kilo plus 100 grammes of flour, 200 grammes of butter, ten eggs, a small glass of rum, a good pinch of salt, 200 grammes of sugar, 20 grammes of yeast and as much milk as required. Put 100 grammes of flour aside. Mix the yeast with a glass of lukewarm water. Put in a warm place for one hour. It will have doubled in volume when it has fermented sufficiently. Put the rest of the flour into a wooden bowl, make a well in the middle and put into it the beaten eggs with the sugar, the melted butter, the rum, salt, yeast and enough milk to make a dough a little less thick than bread dough. Knead the dough. Separate it into four round balls and flatten them. Put them on a board, cover them and keep them warm. The dough will rise until it readily springs back when you put your finger into it. Put the flour on it and cook in a low oven at first, increasing the heat and cooking altogether for thirty to forty-five minutes. Take out the brown buns. They will smell deliciously, and be eaten in next to no time.

Easter is also the time to eat roast lamb, as a symbol of Jesus, the lamb of God. Once a friend of ours invited to her cottage in Périgord a Greek. He very much warmed to the local customs at Easter and decided he would roast a whole lamb on a spit in our friend's meadow. Normally, you would not in Périgord roast a lamb in this way so his approach attracted much curiosity. Laboriously he carried our weighty Périgord fire-dogs into his car and transported them to the meadow. On Easter morning itself he rose early and toiled for most of the day over the open fire, turning the spit incessantly, basting and adding all manner of spices. The finished lamb was delicious. Unfortunately he also set fire to our friend's meadow. This was very much disliked, and the custom has never been repeated.

Traditionally, Périgord Easter lamb, is a boned *gigot* – or leg – with a garlic and herb stuffing. Ask the butcher to remove the bone from a lamb's leg that weighs about two kilos.

🔥

For the stuffing of **Gigot d'agneau farci** mix together eight tablespoonfuls of chopped parsley, one clove of crushed garlic, one teaspoonful of salt and another of pepper, half a teaspoonful of ground rosemary and two tablespoonfuls of chopped shallots. Lay out the boned meat, skin side down, and season with salt and pepper. Spread the stuffing over the lamb and into the pockets left by the bone. Roll the meat into a cylindrical shape, making sure that all the stuffing is inside. Sew up, tying string around the circumference to make sure the meat keeps its shape. Brush with oil and then place in a roasting tin. Put in a pre-heated oven – 450°F. Baste the lamb every five minutes for the first twenty minutes, until it has been browned lightly on all sides. Turn down the oven to 350°F, and roast the lamb for a further 1½ hours or until it is cooked.

As the spring turns to summer, the patronal festivals of village saints begin to be celebrated in the villages throughout the region. Once the clash between farm work and holy days was a serious matter at this time of year. It is said that when a *vigneron* near Orléans refused to honour the festival of St Avitus, which falls inconveniently for farmers on June 17th, but instead worked in his vineyard, the saint, buried nearby, struck him down with a painful illness. Not surprisingly, the religious observance of such festivals has declined dramatically. Eugen Weber traced the fate of a ceremony at La Coquille in north-east Dordogne on the Baptist's patronal festival, June 24th. The Baptist was the patron saint of sheep and shepherds who dubbed Jesus the 'Lamb of God', and each year some 5,000 pilgrims used to gather there to have their sheep blessed by the priest. He, in recompense, would be given forty or fifty young lambs. But by 1900 the priest of La Coquille was receiving scarcely three. In 1920 he was lucky to get a pound of wool.

Some customs survive. I have been told of, but never seen, the present-day customs of St John the Baptist's day, when the priest blesses the people at an open-air mass and bonfires are lit after the traditional herbs of St Jean have been collected: thyme, bay, savory, sweet marjoram, oregano, coriander, parsley, chervil, tarragon, to be dried for use throughout the year.

Nevertheless, the people of the Dordogne still do celebrate the patronal festivals of their village saints during the summer months. They now have to simply take care that they do not eat so much as to totally ruin their ability to do the farm-work. As elsewhere in

France, there is a penchant for long week-end *fêtes* at which solemn crowds watch drum-majorettes, who occasionally dance an inept Parisian can-can. In the evening you can go to a free dance and there will be fireworks, the inevitable games of *boules*, and the ubiquitous *crêpes*. These are, of course, by no means confined to Périgord. But I scarcely need to observe that the cooks of this region serve them, as well as the best chefs elsewhere in France – as thinly as possible, and imaginatively stuffed with such surprising delights as aspara-gus, leeks, and minced duck, as well as the less inspiring chocolate and jam.

🙚

They make **Crêpes** thus. Take 250 grammes of flour, three eggs, a soupspoonful of oil, 250 ml milk, 250 ml water. Mix the flour, eggs, milk, oil and water, adding the salt, and beat with a wooden spoon until the mixture appears clear, like cream. It is vital to prepare this mixture three or four hours before it is needed. Let the *crêpes* fry gently in oil, and serve browned well on both sides. Cut each *crêpe* in half, and cover with either jam or honey. Locally *crêpes* are often flavoured with *anis*, sprinkled with an *eau-de-vie*, or doused in a lethal dose of rum.

Going to *fêtes* is a good way of exploring the Dordogne villages. It is also a reminder of the many saints after whom villages are named, or to whom they are dedicated. Perhaps the most remark-able Dordogne saint is St Front of Périgueux. Legends beyond number surround his life and works. Said to have been baptised by St Peter himself, he was probably a native of the Dordogne and only a spiritual disciple of Peter. He and St George, again according to legend, are alleged to have been among the seventy-two disciples of Jesus who evangelised the Gentiles. Both men set off for Périgord. *En route* St George died; but fortunately St Front at this time was looking after St Peter's staff and miraculously the staff brought George back to life. They then proceeded to Périgord together. A yet more elaborate legend declares that St Front arrived in the Dordogne with seventy-two camels sent to him by the proconsul of Périgord, a Roman named Squirinus who was overcome with remorse at having banished him to Egypt. All this is more or less nonsense. But St Front undoubtedly existed. For many years his bones lay in the cathedral dedicated to him at Périgueux, and pilgrims brought gifts and trade to the city. Protestants in the late sixteenth century threw St Front's body into the River Isle which encircles the city of Périgueux, but his name still has its memorial in the remarkable cathedral there.

Very many villages throughout the *département* were either founded to commemorate saints or dedicated to them: the village of Saint-Agnan, three kilometres from Hautefort and Saint-Amand-de-Coly, with its lovely château, both commemorate early disciples of St Front. The country village of Saint-Georges-de-Montclard near Bergerac, with its eleventh-century chapel and its contemporary old-fashioned market hall, is dedicated to his companion, St Georges. The list could run on literally for pages: Saint-Avit-Sénieur between Cadouin and Beaumont is founded on the spot where, in the sixth century, the Avitus of our cautionary tale concerning the unlucky *vigneron*, built a chapel in honour of the Virgin Mary, while Saint-Capraise-d'Eymet and Saint-Capraise-de-Lalinde, both in wine country, commemorate the learned St Caprais who had been rich and successful before renouncing everything to live a solitary life in Provence, but whose fame was so great that his ambition to live alone proved impossible. Then there are the villages of Saint-Martial-de-Nabirat, where I have my car repaired, and Saint-Martial-Viveyrols, whose names remember the third-century Bishop of Limoges, said by legend to have brought the staff of St Peter to Aquitaine. With it he raised from death the son of a Roman proconsul who had been strangled by a demon and struck blind any pagan priest who dared oppose him. He preached all over Aquitaine, converting many to his faith. One girl named Valeria thereupon also renounced her fiancé, at which he had her beheaded; the girl, it is said, carried her head in her own hands to Martial, before finally dropping down dead.

All these villages share one element of history: they must have been founded or renamed when Christianity was conquering this part of France towards the end of the third century and in the fourth century AD. The barbarians did not give way easily to Christianity. Not surprisingly, then, again and again I have discovered saints whose lives in Périgord proved ones of heroic self-sacrifice.

Vincent of Agen, commemorated at Saint-Vincent-Le-Paluel near Sarlat and Saint-Vincent-de-Cosse, apparently interrupted a druidical feast in his attempts to bring Aquitaine to Christ and was laid out for sacrifice, arms and feet extended and pinned to the ground by stakes, before being savagely scourged and then beheaded. There are architectural reminders of the overlap between Druid and Christian beliefs. Over the west portal of Sarlat cathedral were once carved five remarkable scenes, depicting not Christian saints of the last judgment but the five pagan gods most honoured by the Druids. Minerva was shown inventing both science and the arts; Aesculapius was depicted inventing medicine; Prometheus was carved under siege by an eagle; Atlas carried a huge globe in his right hand; and a fifth scene depicted a God whose name I have been unable to trace, blessing a poor, sick pilgrim.

The small village of Geniès, ten kilometres north of Sarlat, commemorates another saint, St Genesius of Arles. Genesius had been a lawyer before he decided that his profession obliged him to go along with much that he found abhorrent, including laws which persecuted his fellow-Christians. Unable to bear this any longer, according to his biography, one day 'he got up from his seat, flung his registers at the judge's feet and renounced for ever such an evil occupation,' thenceforth living the life of a fugitive until his persecutors finally caught him in Languedoc. He was executed on the banks of the Rhône.

How suitable it is that these early martyrs are now remembered with large quantities of wine and food – as well as rugby-football matches, *ball-trap* (clay-pigeon shooting), cycle racing, motor-rallying and other such recreational passions – is open to debate. Many of the saints believed in privation rather than indulgence. When Avitus who struck down the unfortunate *vigneron* entered a Benedictine Abbey as a lay brother, he was made the cellarer by the abbot. Incredibly, to my mind, Avitus renounced this happy access to good wine and retired to a cave. And when St Caprais, St Honoratus and Honoratus's brother Venentius set off on a pilgrimage to the East, they ate so little that Venentius died in Greece and the two saints were obliged to abandon their pilgrimage.

But I must here voice my strong suspicion that some of the saints of Périgord cheated when it came to abstaining from food. St Cybard, for example, who became a recluse at a monastery at

Saint-Cybard in the second half of the sixth century, supposedly refused to allow the disciples who attached themselves to him to take up manual labour, insisting that they should be constantly at prayer and reminding them of St Jerome's insistence that 'faith never feared hunger'. But – as Butler's useful *Lives of the Saints* records – there was a pleasing let-out for Cybard and his companions: happily, 'he found abundance for himself and his disciples in the beneficence of the faithful, by whom his miracles were greatly appreciated.' And one remembers also that Avitus, who renounced the job of cellarer, was considered by all his contemporaries, except the abbot, to be a simpleton. It was only after the death of the wise abbot that the other monks, realising their folly, found Avitus and forced him back to the monastery to be their new abbot. Not so surprisingly, Avitus ran off to live in the forest.

There is one dish which simply by association reminds me of the saints and early pilgrims who passed through this region on their way to Santiago da Compostela.

&

The ingredients for **Coquilles Saint-Jacques** are six scallops, olive oil, flour, butter, three dessertspoonfuls of cream, six button mushrooms, one chopped shallot, lemon juice, Parmesan cheese and half a glass of Montravel (dry white wine). Clean and cut up the scallops. Marinate for an hour in olive oil and lemon juice. Drain, flour them and cook them gently in butter. Drain. Put them into four shells. Cook the shallots in butter, add the Montravel and a few drops of lemon juice. Reduce. Add the cream and then season. Slice the mushrooms and cook them in butter. Add to the other pan of shallots and cook very gently for a few minutes. Pour over the scallops and grate on some Parmesan cheese. Place under a high grill.

The agricultural festivals which you come across in early September are another good excuse for bucolic and gastronomic celebrations, and the weather will stay mild enough for an open-air feast. One year I noticed, for example, posters advertising the second Ladouze agricultural festival. Ladouze lies twenty kilo-metres south of Périgueux, surrounded by ponds. As a village you could drive through it without stopping, since its treasures – one of which is its fifteenth-century gothic church, with church fonts made from a Gallo-Roman column and fine carved stone fittings – remain hidden from the motorist. The festival's aims were set out on the posters:

To demonstrate new methods of growing tobacco; to show how to dig drains competently; to learn about techniques for coping with forest fires; to present new ways of grinding corn and burning straw.

For these purposes, everyone was invited to sit down to an *entrecôte* lunch between noon and 14.30 hours – and one can be sure that no matter how heated the discussion of agricultural technique, or how many people turned up to eat the *entrecôte*, it would have been excellent.

Now, of course, the purpose of these fairs has become remote from the lives of many of the people of the Dordogne. Once they bound together closely dependent communities. As Karl Marx observed, the French peasants lived 'like potatoes in a sack'. Each peasant community was a social entity, just like any other, but keeping itself to itself, with families in each community knowing each other face to face and relying on each other for protection and mutual help. Today, many of these communities have died. In the last 125 years the *département* has lost a quarter of its population: 500,000 people inhabited Périgord in the middle of the nineteenth century, but today that population stands at only 373,000. In fact, when the government set up the gunpowder factory at Bergerac, so few workers were available in this region that some had to be brought in from as far away as Brest and Alsace-Lorraine.

Exactly why the population began to decline when it did is unclear. Until the mid-nineteenth century peak of 1851 the population was actually growing. Then, for reasons demographers find hard to discover, the population began to fall. This was a time when men and women were optimistic that good times were coming. Few could foresee that the profitable river trade was almost at an end. No-one then remotely anticipated the devastation phylloxera was to bring, destroying completely parts of the wine trade in the second half of the century, or the steady fragmentation of farms following Napoleon's Civil Code, which abolished primogeniture and substituted equal shares for all descendants. One explanation could be that the population began to fall as a response to the rising expectations produced by greater prosperity.

That fall has been accompanied by an extraordinary shift out of the countryside. The destruction of the vines meant that those parts of the region with the poorest soil and the poorest communications were the first to be abandoned. For many emigration was the only way of finding a decent livelihood, and the experience of military service between 1914 and 1918 accelerated this. Unable to feed large families, people stopped having them. Until 1946 births only exceeded deaths in the years 1921 to 1926. Those who did not wish to leave the *département* were strongly tempted to move to find work in the towns. As a result the size of larger communities has grown enormously. Ribérac, with a population of 3,607 in 1876, now has a population of over 4,000; Bergerac, which housed 13,120 people in 1876, had nearly twice that number in 1962; Périgueux's population over the same period grew from 24,000 to 41,000. Some smaller towns, such as Neuvic-sur-l'Isle and Thiviers have also increased in size, partly because of their importance in being on the route to Paris. The fall in the countryside and small villages has therefore been far more dramatic than the overall figure suggests. In winter, when most of the trees are without leaves, you can see how many people once lived in uninhabited areas. Half-concealed in the woods are deserted, shut up, often ruined houses.

The statistics speak for themselves. But it is still easy to overlook the extent of the cultural changes, in particular the loss of regional identity. In 1863 fully a third of Dordogne children could still speak no French. The following year school inspectors found patois 'in general use' throughout the region and, in spite of the determined efforts of teachers to suppress it as part of the national policy of centralism, 'as indestructible as the air breathed in each locality'. Even as late as 1880 an inspector declared that 'the obstinate indifference to French' in this *département* would not be overcome for another generation. It was in reaction to the central goverment's efforts to stamp out regional culture that the Félibrée movement was founded in 1854 at Fontségugne, near Avignon, by men and women made newly conscious of the subtle literature and music produced by the people of the Langue d'Oc over many centuries.

Over exactly the same period that has witnessed the prolonged crisis of the countryside, and in particular in recent years, it has flourished.

Each year sixty-five festivals are arranged throughout the Dordogne to revive the old folklore. Dressed in traditional costume, men and women gather to dance the old dances of the region, to sing Langue d'Oc songs, to cherish their old culture. In 1978, 26,000 people gathered for the celebrations at Excideuil and the following year an astonishing 40,000 came together to honour the Langue d'Oc at Brantôme. Those figures reflect the strength of attachment to a cherished, if threatened, regional identity – and they help also to explain the self-conscious appreciation of regional food and the special emphasis placed on continuity of cooking tradition. At a time of very rapid social change and adjustment, that is of far greater importance than has often been understood.

The Waters of the Dordogne

'The Dordogne here and the Vézère not far away,
mirror the present and the past. On their banks, we
who endure for a day contemplate the images of
eternity.'

ALBÉRIC CAHUET

Around the great rivers of the Dordogne grew up a civilisation in total contrast to the severe plateaux of the region. On either side of the rivers men and women have lived for centuries, cultivating the land, building manors, châteaux and farms. A ship-building trade grew up beside the Dordogne. Coopers with apprentices plied their trade. Merchants built houses by the riverside. Ferrymen proliferated. So did hotels and, later, restaurants, benefitting from the assets of fishing, a water-mill to grind corn and the proximity of river transport.

Once the chief river highways – the Dronne, the Vézère, the Dropt, but especially the Dordogne and the Isle – carried a rich trade. Boats almost invariably descended the Dordogne and ascended the Isle. They carried down to Bordeaux wood, juniper berries, wine, straw and paper. There they would be broken up and their planks used again. These light boats dismembered thus when the journey was over were called *argentats*; *couraux* were flat boats driven by paddles, oars and punt poles, well-adapted for traversing shallows; *filadières* were long, narrow speedy fishing boats.

Heavier boats were used for returning up the river, tacking from side to side, sometimes as many as twenty times, towed by patient horses or even gangs of men, carrying salt, sea fish (dried and salted), sugar and other provisions for a lean and hungry people. From June to September it was possible to sail back along the Dordogne as far as Bergerac. In winter you could reach Souillac – a good boat could make the journey in seven days – and in both directions the river traffic carried the product of forges, chestnuts and wine. But Bergerac was the chief port, and Libourne was where the river traffic met seafaring vessels.

There were many natural hazards. Navigators had to avoid shallows, rocks, submerged trees. They coped with theft, loss of ships and lives, breakage. Most bridges over the Dordogne were not built before the nineteenth century. Those built earlier were often flimsy or hazardous. Take the bridges over the Isle at Périgueux. The first to be built was the Pont Tourrepiche, with three fine arches. It fell down in 1375. One arch was rebuilt in 1435, then in 1612 a master architect named Nicolas Rambourg rebuilt the whole bridge. Another one was built below it in 1718 (here bread was given to the poor and the city executioner plied his trade). This bridge caused flooding every winter, because it dammed the flow of the river, so the citizens demolished it in 1860. The municipality ordered the Pont de la Cité to be built in 1832, contracting to pay the builder by tolls. He made a bad bargain, since hardly anybody would pay to use it. Next to this was a twelfth-century bridge called the Pont du Talon, which became so rickety that it had to be pulled down in 1821. At Bergerac the great flood of March 1783 submerged the bridge on March 9th by 4 p.m., and by nine that evening the bridge had collapsed. Trees were carried away from either bank of the river. The Duke of Luynes lost beasts, several houses and much furniture. People took refuge on the high ground, driving their beasts before them. Despite these problems and natural hazards the river trade was profitable.

Now, however, all this has disappeared. The main blow was the coming of the railways. Tentative attempts to dredge the Dordogne in the nineteenth century were mostly abandoned. In 1900 ninety-four boats still plied the river, carrying over 16,000 tons of cheese, coal, charcoal, firewood and timber for casks as far as Bordeaux. But this was the last gasp of a dying trade.

Today the economic significance of the great rivers of Périgord is threefold. Firstly, they provide hydro-electricity. Secondly, they attract the tourist. My younger daughter has a boat, and regularly swings down the steep path to the river so she can sail placidly around the *cingle*, or loop, here to the foot of château Montfort. Then I have to drive down and bring her and the boat back again. More commercially, all along the river in the tourist season, vans trip up the river with kayaks and hire them out to holidaymakers who sail down the Dordogne, to be brought home again in these same vans later in the day.

Thirdly, they provide fish. For centuries – since the first saints – the people of this region have eaten, unfailingly, the fruits and fish of the rivers. And still, from the early morning till dusk, men lean over the bridges that cross the river, staring intently far below to where their lines tempt the carp, trout, eels and gudgeon. Most people, however, usually buy their fish and seafood from the market stalls. As elsewhere in France, a high proportion will be locally fished and sold fresh rather than frozen. Here much of it is brought directly from the Atlantic coast: Bordeaux, Saint-Jean-de-Luz and the oyster beds of the Arcachon. Other very popular fish – carp and pike for example – which were unfamiliar delicacies to me until I started to live in Périgord, are fished from the rivers, or, like trout and *écrevisses* – fresh water crayfish – those delicate, delightful little crustaceans, farmed. Two other types of seafood and fish far more readily available and more frequently eaten than one might expect, are lobster and lamprey – the latter a river or sea eel which is usually cooked in wine-based stews. Prawns, lobsters and crayfish are often sold live. However, I have assumed in recipes that all fish and seafood is fresh but killed.

Over the centuries the people of Périgord have evolved delicious methods of cooking these fish. To my mind there are two regional dishes which are, in their own way, masterpieces of simplicity. Small fish, such as gudgeons, roach, little perch, bleak, barbel, little eels and countless others are used to make a simple but great delicacy of small, crisply fried fish, traditionally eaten with the fingers, very quickly, while the fish remain hot.

It is a mistake to think that fish for **Friture péri-gourdine** is simply fried. Cleaned and washed, the fish is first cooked in oil *without being rolled first in flour*. Then just before they are eaten, they are heated in fresh oil in another frying pan, being cut smaller if necessary, there to be enhanced by means of a clove of garlic, parsley, salt and pepper. They are served with vinegar.

The old tradition of frying without a flour coating is not everywhere observed these days. Some cookery books even give complicated recipes for mixing a substance fit to roll the fish in. But the ordinary housewife, the peasant kitchen, the informed hotel would have no truck with this sort of thing. One exception might be allowed: some distinguish between the *friture de goujons* – comprising fish smaller than 10 cm in length – and the medium *friture* – which can include fish up to 25 cm in length, weighing maybe 150 grammes. In the latter case people often dip the fish in milk, salt it and then roll it in flour.

If you have got a flour coating you must make sure the oil is hot, but not too hot. Gradually increase the temperature as the fishes fry. It is important not to create too thick a crust until the final moments. Some cooks make light incisions in the fishes' stomachs to make it easier for them to fry all through. A medium-sized *friture* is garnished with a clove of chopped garlic, some fried parsley and the juice of unripe grapes, and these days cutlery arrives with both small and medium-sized *fritures* in restaurants. Some of them would, no doubt, look somewhat askance upon the traditional finger method.

The other traditional recipe which I consider a masterpiece is *stockfish*, a speciality of the region around Figeac, which is close to the famous salt-cod dish, *brandade de morue*, but far more subtle since the fish used – *le stockfish* – is only very lightly salted. This is now considered a gourmet delicacy in Paris, but here it is still family food, eaten with a spoon as it has been for centuries. The mild *stockfish* was first brought here by Norwegian merchants, when Figeac was an important wool town in the late middle ages. Then salting was essential as a preservative, but recently, with refrigeration, fresh cod has become more popular.

♣

The ingredients for **Gâteau de cabillaud périgourdin**, made with fresh cod rather than *le stockfish*, could not be

more straightforward. You need a kilo of cod, three
eggs, a kilo of potatoes, four cloves of garlic, six
soupspoonfuls of oil, pepper and parsley. Place the cod in
cold water and bring to the boil. As soon as the water
boils, cover the pan, remove from the heat and leave for
twenty minutes. Drain the fish and put in the water in
which it has been cooking the potatoes, cut into quarters.
Let them cook for twenty minutes. During this time
crumble the cod with a fork and place it in an oven-dish,
along with half of the oil and the chopped parsley and
garlic. Work the mixture till it becomes creamy. Make a
purée of the potatoes. Season. Work the yolks of the eggs
into the purée. Mix into the cod, adding also the egg
whites. Brush the top of this with the rest of the oil and
cook in a well-heated oven for half an hour. Serve in the
dish in which it has been cooked.

You may still find a *gâteau de morue périgourdin*, made with salt-cod,
which will have a much stronger flavour, or it may be found in
restaurants served with tomato sauces that suggest a Basque
influence.

Two other recipes, both taught to me by my neighbour, Mme
Véril Moïse, are characteristically simple but succulent dishes for
trout and carp, which are found everywhere in this region. In both the
fish is left whole and given an economic stuffing or filling with plenty
of flavour. I learned the first recipe as the result of a mutually
appreciated joke. One day I was resting on the wall of our house that
fronts the narrow path from the woods when M. and Mme Véril
Moïse came walking past. He was carrying a plastic bag containing
two carp. We shook hands, and he politely asked what I had been
doing that day. I replied that most of the day I had been typing a
chapter in a book about the life and teaching of Jesus. 'I can see,' I
added, 'that you have been fishing.' Without a second's pause he
replied, 'Fishing, yes; but I am not a Fisher of Men!' Exceedingly
pleased with this joke, he then suggested we come later for a drink. So
we did.

🔥

Mme Véril was cooking the two cleaned fish. For her
Carpe farcie, she made a stuffing with finely crumbled

bread, a handful of *morilles*, an egg and some thyme. Then she cooked the fish. With the juice in which they had cooked she made a sauce, adding chopped shallots, parsley and a spoonful of mustard.

When it was time for the Vérils to eat, they insisted we stay a little longer and drink just one more glass of wine. Strangely (in the eyes of so-called connoisseurs outside France), they were drinking red wine as an accompaniment to the carp. I could scarcely contain my hunger. Red wine also goes well with fish stuffed with diced *jambon* and mushrooms, another favourite way of serving carp, trout or pike in Périgord.

The second recipe I learned by walking into their kitchen to find a delicious and intriguing smell wafting from two trout sizzling in the pan.

Mme Véril was making **Truite au verjus**. Chop three cloves of garlic and two soupspoonfuls of parsley. Peel two bunches of green grapes and remove the pips. Clean and wash the trout. Put into each trout some grapes, some garlic, parsley, salt and pepper; you should keep back some garlic and parsley. Roll each trout in flour. Heat some oil in a pan and add 75 grammes of fatty bacon. Allow the bacon to cook a little and then add the trout, two at a time. Turn the fish gently to try and avoid breaking the skin. When they are cooked, remove them from the pan and place them on absorbent paper, and then on a serving dish. Put the remaining grapes into the frying pan and cook quickly for two or three minutes before putting them around the trout. Sprinkle the remaining garlic and parsley over the fish and serve.

The five chief rivers – the Dronne, the Vézère, the Dropt, the Isle and the Dordogne itself – flow towards the south-west, more or less parallel to each other, following the natural fall of the *département*. The great Dordogne itself, 290 miles long, derives its name from *Duranna*, a Celtic word meaning swift waters. The mildest of the rivers as well as the most majestic, it can be deceptively placid in this area, claiming half a dozen victims by drowning each year. The first time we ever came to Périgord we drove by way of Souillac and, following this beautiful river, found ourselves suddenly entranced by it.

Sheila Steen described the river at Domme perfectly in 1949:

'Surely, I thought on those June days, the Dordogne must be the quietest river in the world. It lay shining in the hot, still air. A few boys and men sat tranquilly fishing. A few women, barefooted, wearing chip hats, slapped their wet laundry with lumps of strong-smelling, yellow Marseilles soap on the boards at the water's edge. Swallows flew low. Now and then the plop of a fish sounded loudly. The trees shimmered, argent, silent. The children paddled; their movements sent out smooth luminous rings on the water. . . . Other children played up and down them like butterflies, hovering. Their cries seemed swaddled in the gleaming heat and quiet.'

Domme is now a noted gastronomical centre. There you can eat delicious mussels. They are by no means unique to this region but they are very good.

This is how you cook **Moules marinières** as they are eaten in Périgord, made with olive oil rather than butter and with the juices unthickened. Take five litres of fresh mussels, olive oil, four chopped shallots, some parsley, a sprig of thyme, a bay leaf, some black pepper, 250 ml of white wine and a little salt. Scrub the mussels, removing all the hairs, mud, etc. Wash them in plenty of water, discarding any mussels that are cracked or open. Drain them. Heat the oil in a pan and fry the shallots until they are soft. Add the herbs, pepper and the wine; then add the mussels. Cover and cook quickly, shaking the pan until the mussels open. Remove the mussels from the pan and discard the empty half of each one. Keep them warm in a serving dish. Boil the remaining juices until they are reduced to half and pour over the mussels. Sprinkle with the chopped parsley. If you do want to thicken the sauce, make a *beurre manié* from 25 grammes of butter and a tablespoonful of flour. Drop this – a teaspoonful at a time – into the stock, and stir until it thickens.

Upstream from Domme at Carlux, there is a château half-destroyed by the English during the Hundred Years' War and never rebuilt. Here are, unusually for the Dordogne, lime trees. And here they cook a special dish with the local pike.

§

To cook **Brochet à la Carlux** you need to buy a pike weighing 1½ kilos, 125 grammes of mushrooms and 125 grammes of sorrel. You also need a sprig of tarragon, chopped parsley, two shallots, salt and pepper, 500 ml of white wine, a cupful of flour, two eggs, 100 grammes of butter and breadcrumbs. Remove the fins, but not the head, from the pike, clean and wash it inside and out and dry on absorbent paper. Clean the sorrel and remove the main stalks. Remove the stalks of the mushrooms, wash them and cut them into fine slices. Wash the shallots and chop them finely. In a flameproof dish heat a little oil and brown the pike on all sides. Salt and pepper the fish. Pour over the white wine and add the shallots, sorrel, mushrooms and herbs. Season. Cover the dish with tinfoil. Cook over medium heat for about one hour. A little water may have to be added from time to time. Remove the mushrooms and the herbs. Put them into a bowl and add the beaten eggs. Stir in the flour. Mix until the paste has a smooth consistency. Then place it into the interior of the pike. Spoon off the juices that are in the casserole into another, smaller saucepan. Place this on a low heat and add the butter, a little at a time. Put the pike into this sauce, along with the breadcrumbs, and cook for another ten minutes on a hot flame. Serve.

The Dordogne here is fond of making great wide loops – they are known locally as *cingles* – and here, near our home, is one of the most pronounced, the *cingle de Montfort* with its extraordinary medieval château. The river flows on, its power growing all the time. At nearby Cénac the average rate of flow is 21 litres a second. Just after château Montfort, at Daglan, the tributary Léon adds its waters and fish, and further downstream other Périgord rivers also join the Dordogne.

In particular, the River Vézère joins it at Limeuil. Here, where the view is 'the most beautiful in Périgord' according to Eugène Le Roy, two stone bridges with round arches stand at right angles to each other, spanning the Dordogne and the Vézère. Limeuil is immensely seductive in summer. In the distance are green fields merging into gentle blue hills. The vines that grow as canopies over many of the houses are leafy. Peasants stroll in their berets. And the locals fish fat carp from their two rivers.

Carp has a very creamy flesh which lends itself well to rich stuffings. It tends to be bony, and it is therefore a good idea to ask the fishmonger to remove the whole backbone for you. The gastronome Curnonsky particularly admired Dordogne carp stuffed with *pâté de foie gras*, which I first ate here. This is Curnonsky's recipe:

🔥

> For **Carpe farcie au foie gras** for six people dice some *pâté de foie gras* – not too small, though. Season with salt and pepper and flavour with two tablespoons of cognac. Clean and skin a carp weighing about 1½ to 2 kilos. Stuff it with the *foie gras*, then stud the fish with a chopped up truffle and wrap with strips of fat bacon. Bake the fish in a slow oven, set at 325°F, for forty minutes. Garnish it when served with slices of *foie gras* topped with a thin slice of truffle.

I have also read that carp are very good stuffed with chestnuts, but I have never tasted this.

From Limeuil, the valley of the Vézère snakes northwards towards the Limousin. In 1899 Eugène Le Roy watched it flowing slowly, 'held back by a series of locks, and gleaming like a massive snake with silver scales between its varied banks of green fields, bare bends, and slopes bearing trees and vines.' What Le Roy did not know was that this gentle river slaked the thirst of our earliest ancestors. Prehistoric man made his home here. These men and women, hunters and gatherers, never mastered the art of writing. But they were astonishing artists, painting the walls of their caves with long-extinct animals, carving into the rock face bison and Siberian leopards who once roamed this area of the Dordogne, sculpting and scratching the outlines of mammoths and ibex, drawing strange hunting scenes that scholars still try to decipher.

Over sixty caves, once inhabited by these artists and hunters, have been discovered in the Vézère valley, alongside more than 150 shelters, dug out of the rocks, where they made their homes. The most famous are those at Lascaux, but they are now closed to all save scholars to try and prevent deterioration. At nearby Montignac, they serve excellent, quickly cooked shrimp from the Atlantic coast.

Crevettes aux ciboulettes take no more than fifteen minutes to prepare. For three or four persons you need 200 grammes of fresh shrimps, 40 ml of oil, four sprigs of chives, salt and pepper. Chop the chives, carefully wash and drain the shrimps. Throw them with the chives in the hot oil, stirring frequently. Serve hot, with good bread.

Just downstream of the junction between the Dordogne and the Vézère, the river makes a second wonderful *cingle*, at Trémolat. The spectacular, dramatic landscape was perfectly used as a backdrop by Claude Chabrol, master of *film noir*, in *Le Boucher* and our visitors often like to visit the small town. On one such trip, we discovered this Dordogne recipe for lobster, cooked in a fresh tomato sauce like the famous dish of Provençal origin, *Homard à l'américaine*, but with the addition of maize to the *court-bouillon* and goose fat and cognac to the sauce. In the *logis*, a napkin tucked into our shirt collars as if we were schoolchildren likely to make a mess of our clean clothes, we tucked in.

For **Homard à la périgourdine**, boil a *court-bouillon*, well-seasoned with onions, carrots and herbs, including some maize. Throw in two lobsters and cook for a quarter of an hour. Crush 1¼ kilos of tomatoes and put them in a saucepan with salt, pepper, a clove of garlic, some thyme, a bay leaf and small onions. Cook thoroughly. In

another saucepan put some goose fat and a spoonful of
flour. Strain the tomatoes into this mixture, stirring well
until you have a smooth sauce. Cut up the lobster and put
it into this sauce. Add a small glass of cognac and a clove
of garlic cut up into pieces. The dish tastes infinitely
better, so they say, if it is cooked the day before you eat it
and heated up again before serving.

As the Dordogne flows on, it continues to be joined by many
little streams: the Couze at Montferrand-du-Périgord, the Nauze at
Belvès, the Caudeau at Bergerac. The ample river here, with its
ancient bridge, once teemed with traffic; and since east-west roads
crossed north-south routes, the town developed into an important
commercial centre. You can see high on a wall of the Rue du Port at
Bergerac marks where the river flooded in the past. The highest the
waters reached was over thirteen metres above the bank, on 20
January 1728. More recently, on 20 February 1957 the flood waters
rose to nearly ten metres.

In the Place du Marché Couvert, vegetables, cheeses, oysters,
sole and those eel-like, flat-headed, bearded fresh-water fish which
we call sometimes burbot and sometimes devil-fish (the French call
them *lotte*) are on sale. In the Bergeraçois region, if it is springtime,
you often find on the menus salmon and lampries. I once ate some
excellent salmon cutlets cooked in a *béchamel* sauce. When I got back
home I looked up the recipe.

♦

For **Côtelettes de saumon**, take 300 grammes of
cooked salmon, 100 grammes of mushrooms, 30
grammes of truffles, chopped finely, and mixed in with
300 ml of *béchamel* sauce that has been thickened with two
egg yolks. Leave the sauce to cool. Divide the salmon
into four portions each weighing 75 grammes, and shape
them into *côtelettes*, binding with a few tablespoons of the
béchamel. Coat them in beaten egg and cover with
breadcrumbs. Fry gently for a few minutes and serve
with the sauce.

Écrevisses are also eaten a great deal in this region. They are slightly difficult crustaceans to prepare, since you have to cut them in two, remove their thin black intestines and cut away the little sacs in their heads. It is easier, of course, to enjoy them in restaurants instead of preparing them yourself; but since you can often find them on sale – and cheap – in the markets of Périgord, it is also worth while finding out at least one of the ways they are cooked in this region. A *sauce bordelaise* is usually based on red wine, but for fish white wine is often used.

For **Écrevisses à la bordelaise** you need 230 grammes of butter, a soupspoonful of flour, two carrots, a large onion, ten shallots, a clove of garlic, a *bouquet garni* made from tarragon, a bay leaf and thyme, salt and pepper, two soupspoonfuls of chopped parsley, a bottle of Bergerac *blanc sec* and a small glass of cognac. Cook gently for ten minutes, in 100 grammes of butter, the finely chopped carrots, shallots and garlic. Then add twenty crayfish, cooking them until they are quite red. Pour over the cognac, and flambé. Take the crayfish out of the casserole, and add to it the white wine, *bouquet garni*, salt and pepper Reduce for five minutes. Return the crayfish and cook for twelve to fifteen minutes more. Prepare a sauce with the remaining butter, flour and cooking liquor. Serve the crayfish, pouring over them this sauce and sprinkling with chopped parsley.

Downstream from Bergerac, the river flows majestically through the *bastide* of Sainte-Foy-la-Grande with its marvellous grid-like pattern of streets, before finally reaching Libourne where in the old days the river traffic met seafaring vessels. Here the Dordogne is finally joined by the waters of the Isle and its tributary, the Dronne, before running on towards Bordeaux. The River Dronne flows through some of the most productive parts of the *département*, above all at Brantôme. Here, they serve delicious trout with almonds. Trout are now extensively farmed in this region, but I do not recommend their flavour or fattiness compared to a good river trout.

❧

For **Truite de rivière aux amandes** cooked this way
you need four trout, olive oil, salt and pepper, 50
grammes of skinned almonds and the juice of one small
lemon. Clean the trout but leave on the heads. Season the
cavity and skins with salt and pepper. Heat the oil in a
frying pan and fry the trout on each side for about six
minutes until golden brown and cooked through.
Remove the trout from the pan. Place them on a serving
dish, but keep them warm. Fry the almonds in the pan
until they, too, are golden. Add the lemon juice and pour
over the fish.

But there are many more unusual recipes for trout in this region –
in fact, there are nearly as many recipes as chefs. They are quite
often stuffed with meat of some kind – one of the many *rillettes*,
pâtés or *confits*.

❧

The owner and chef of the Hôtel l'Esplanade in Domme
arrogantly recommends his own **Truite braisée au
Bergerac sec**. His arrogance is justified. It is excellent.
This is how he cooks it. Clean four trout and season with
salt and pepper. Butter a deep fireproof baking dish and
sprinkle on the bottom a tablespoonful of finely chopped
shallots, along with some thyme and parsley. Arrange
the trout on top, covering with greaseproof paper that
you have lightly buttered. Pour over the trout enough
Bergerac *blanc sec* to cover them. Cook gently in a
moderate oven for about twenty minutes. Then place the
trout on a serving dish, keeping them warm. Heat the
juices that remain in the fireproof dish, until they are
reduced to two-thirds of their original volume. Add 175
ml of cream, and reduce a little more. Stirring, add 50
grammes of butter. Pass this sauce through a sieve and
pour around the trout.

The waters of the Isle have contributed to a tradition of excellent
fish dishes.

Carpe à la Neuvic takes its name from Neuvic on the River Isle, south-west of Périgueux, a town with a sixteenth-century château close by the river. To make this delicious rich dish you will need for six people a carp weighing two kilos, 400 grammes fillet of pork, 300 grammes *foie gras* (from a goose), a tin of truffles weighing 125 grammes, 100 grammes of breadcrumbs, an egg, two shallots, salt and pepper, a glass of cognac, a glass of Madeira, 500 ml white wine, 75 grammes of butter, *bouquet garni*, a carrot, an onion and parsley. Clean the carp, removing the fins. Wash it inside and out. Dry. Mince the pork, the *foie gras* and the shallots. Drain the truffles and cut up as finely as possible. Add this to the stuffing along with the juice from the tin and the breadcrumbs. Mix in the egg and the brandy, salt and pepper. Put this stuffing into the carp and sew it up. Place in an oiled casserole. Put the chopped carrot, onion and *bouquet garni* underneath. Pour over the Madeira and the wine, adding some *noisettes* of butter. Cook on medium heat for one hour, adding a little liquid from time to time. Remove the string from the carp and serve on a dish garnished with the chopped parsley. Pour the juices that are left in the casserole through a sieve and serve as an accompaniment to the sauce.

At Périgueux, the capital of the *département*, which lies to the east of Neuvic, I have been served an excellent fillet of brill – *barbue* –which I presume was caught in the River Isle. The *filets* were fried in oil with crushed tomatoes, chopped shallots, and savory. Then they had moistened the fish with white wine and poached it in a covered dish. With the bones of the brill they had made a broth, greatly reduced and with the liquor of the fish added to it. The finished dish was served with mushrooms that had been cooked in oil.

At the restaurant *Le Domino* there, I have eaten juicy *langoustines à l'oignon*.

For **Langoustines à l'oignon** take 800 grammes of prawns, two onions, two shallots, a carrot, two soupspoonfuls of tomato purée, a large glass of Bergerac *blanc sec*, 70 grammes of butter, some parsley, a glass of cognac, salt and pepper. Peel the vegetables, dice them finely; chop the parsley and wash the prawns. Melt half the butter in a frying pan and add the vegetables. When they are golden, add the prawns and sauté them for four minutes. Flambé them with the cognac. Next pour over the glass of white wine and add the tomato purée; salt and pepper and cook for ten minutes over a hot flame. Remove the prawns and reduce the sauce, adding the rest of the butter. Pour the sauce over the prawns and serve hot, sprinkled with parsley.

As the river flows on towards the great port of Bordeaux, it leaves behind the *département* of the Dordogne. Towards the estuary lie the famous *claires*, or oyster-beds, from which come the oysters our neighbours always eat on New Year's Eve and at other celebrations. I would give no recipes for this, only Mme Véril's golden rule for the success of all fish cookery: that the fish should find their way to the table as quickly as possible.

Les Trois Périgords: A Short Tour

'The work of the artists of Périgord is, even in the
smallest ways, characterised by three qualities that
make it special – variety, the unexpected and a
horror of banality.'

JULES DE VERNEILH

The skills of the French butcher are remarkable, and that of the
Dordogne butcher legendary. Henry Miller, the American novelist, visiting Sarlat just before the outbreak of World War II, was
amazed by the butcher's techniques: 'the grace and tenderness of
his knife-stroke, the almost maternal tenderness with which he
carried a quarter of veal from the chopping block to the marble
slab in the window.'

The tradition continues in the countless local butchers of
Périgord, although it is slightly lost, alas, in the burgeoning
supermarkets, where meat tends increasingly to appear pre-
packed. My own butcher, M. Lambert of Domme, assisted by his
son Bernard, presents his customers with a daily performance –
there is no other word for it – as he cuts, packs, creates and
presents superb pieces of meat with a flourish and sense of theatre.
Once M. Lambert's toe was broken when a cow trod on him at
the abattoir. He tremendously enjoyed limping around in his
shop, explaining, to anyone who asked, exactly how the toe was
progressing towards recovery. I think he would forgive me if I
suggest that the toe's agonies were more than a little prolonged, in
the interest of theatrical creativity.

Another time I decided to do nothing for a day, and went with a friend to a café in a village on the road between Sarlat and Souillac. We discovered that the local butcher and his wife were in a rage with each other. After serving each customer, the butcher crossed the road to the café, bought us all a drink, and gave an account of the latest stage in the impending divorce. As soon as he saw another customer approaching his shop he excused himself, darted back and served – no doubt giving the customer yet more details of the play. As the day drew to a close he appeared once more in the café, wreathed in smiles, and announced that the divorce was off.

There are certain notable differences from butchers' shops elsewhere. Because everything is. prepared in your presence, naturally you wait longer for your turn. No-one complains. They are rewarded by superbly cut meat and sage advice on how to cook whatever you have bought. You ask for, say, 1¾ to 2 kilos of rolled topside of beef. The butcher shows you his available cuts and you choose. He asks what you intend to cook and carefully, maternally, he slices the beef exactly as it needs to be for the dish and the number of people who will be eating it. It may initially seem expensive. But you are being sold nothing more and nothing less than what you asked for: no useless bones, no unnecessary fat, no inedible gristle. Even a humble beefburger, *boeuf haché*, is made before your very eyes from fine cuts – so that you know you are not being sold a mixture of cheapest cuts, sawdust, ground up pigs' hooves and all manner of sweepings-up. In this sense, the meat is supremely good value.

The quality of meat is commented upon by nearly all our visitors. Once, just after Christmas, we were joined in Périgord by a clergyman who was exhausted by what he had just done over the Christmas season. To cheer him up we went on an outing by way of Bergerac to Sainte-Foy-la-Grande, eating lunch *en route* in a simple working men's restaurant. There was one menu, no more, with the *plat du jour* that day named as *bifteck* – a dish, incidentally, introduced into France only during the Anglomania of the restored monarchy (the word was adopted by the Académie Française in 1835). It was served swimming in blood, to my mind beautifully cooked, but I wondered if my clerical friend quite agreed given the English preference for shrivelled meat. However, he seemed to empty his plate with considerable speed. Only when we arrived back at our village did he take out of his pocket a plastic bag with the bloody piece of beef inside. Without saying a word he took out a frying pan and re-cooked it. As he ate it, his face creased in smiles, he observed that the steak was far too good a cut and quality to have been thrown away.

Veal is still probably the favourite meat throughout the Dordogne. Often a piece is cut as a *rouelle* from the beast's thigh, with the bone still in the middle to preserve all the juices. The customer likes a thick piece, weighing two kilos or more. I am told they used to cook it preferably on a fire made from vine shoots. Well-oiled, salted and peppered, one side would be thoroughly cooked. Salt and pepper would be added to the other side before the *rouelle* was turned over in the heat. The cooked veal would be served with *verjus*, the juice of unripened grapes.

It is a joy to watch a French butcher creating cuts of beef. He slices away the undercut in one piece. He creates *entrecôtes* from the flesh around the ribs of the animal. *Faux filet* is derived from the uppercut of the loin. *Tournedos* derives from the tail of the undercut. Often, beef is not sold by cut, but according to the recipe described by a customer. Most butchers also make *bouillon* themselves and sell it in plastic bottles for next-to-nothing. To buy it ready-made like this saves a lot of cooking time.

But Périgord is not a region powerfully devoted to raising cattle. In the early 1980s the entire *département* of 922,505 hectares devoted no more than 79,000 hectares to producing fodder. Dordogne farmers breed far more milk cows than animals destined for the butchers' slabs. No more than 33,000 beef cattle are produced a year, and most of these come from the southern area known as Périgord *vert*. Five times that number of sheep graze on its hillsides, and three times as many pigs are raised by Dordogne farmers. In every butcher's shop you will find not only fine cuts of pork but also pig's trotters, used to thicken the juices of *daubes* and casseroles. You will also find the local maize-fed chickens with their plump yellow flesh and the fat turkeys brought in from Toulouse.

The butchers' shops are often exquisitely tiled, both inside and out, usually in the lush style of the Second Empire. I often wonder why the related *charcuterie* are by contrast so much like any other shop – leaving aside, of course, their mouth-watering windows. The *traiteurs* of Sarlat and Périgueux were famed for their pork

products from the eighteenth century, and the array of *pâtés*,
sausages and cooked meats is still astonishing. *Boudin noir*, as well as
boudin blanc, has been a speciality of the Dordogne for quite as long
as it has been relished by Lancashire folk. In fact, despite my
childhood loyalties, I long ago gave up believing the figment of
Lancastrian pride that 'black puddings', made principally of pigs'
blood, had been invented in the town of Bury. Although black
pudding is excellent simply poached, usually these days they are
served with apples. The *boudins* are gently fried, turning them
frequently. The apples, peeled and diced, are also fried. When they
are cooked, a dash of vinegar is added. The *boudins* are then sliced
and served along with the apple and usually also mashed potatoes.

Although *rillettes* are not considered a great speciality of this
region, they are widely eaten and made, sometimes with the
addition of goose. *Rillettes* are something like a coarse *pâté*, a highly
seasoned, minced pork. They come in jars, with a knife stuck into
them. You eat them as you eat *pâté de foie gras*, not vulgarly with a
fork but put on to slices of bread with a knife.

> **Rillettes de porc** are not difficult to make. You need a
> kilo of boned pork from the pig's belly, 350 grammes of
> pork fat, two crushed cloves of garlic, two teaspoonfuls
> of chopped parsley, two tablespoonfuls of Bergerac
> *blanc sec*, and salt.
> Cut off any rind from the pork, rub it with salt and
> leave for half a day. Chop into small pieces, adding cubed
> fat, wine, crushed garlic and parsley. Mix well, put in an
> ovenproof dish and cook for four hours at 275°F. Drain
> off the fat and keep it. Shred the mixture with a fork, not
> too finely, and pour it into clean jam jars. Use the fat to
> preserve the *rilletes* by sealing the top of each jar with a
> thin layer. Keep refrigerated, but leave at room temper-
> ature for an hour or so before serving.

I relish *rilletes* – though I have to confess that to do so I had to
realise that this dish is *not* an inferior *pâté*. Also known as *grillons*, in
this region, they are very good thickly spread on bread for
lunchtime sandwiches.

Alongside the *boudins* and *rillettes* will be countless other *pâtés*, *jambons*, *saucisses* and *galantines*. Another speciality are the *ballotines* for which the bird is boned, stuffed with forcemeat, simmered in stock and then allowed to go cold. When cold it is coated with a white sauce, glazed in jelly and then, if it is to be preserved, bottled away. Finally, of course, at the most expensive end of the products, will be the *conserves* enriched with *foie gras*. They are worth trying at least once during a visit since they are so far superior to canned products sold outside the region.

One of the pleasures I find in eating in Périgord is to savour what, according to the menu, ought to be the same dish throughout the region. In fact each part of this *département* can bring its own quiddity to a dish: even twenty minutes' driving makes for subtle gastronomic differences. Take, for example, a simple *entrecôte*. The butcher will have cut away any gristle or surplus fat, and he will also – if he is true to his trade – have lightly beaten the meat with the side of his meat cleaver. The meat will usually be grilled, though sometimes in this region it is fried. Beyond that there are endless different variations. Often they make a mushroom sauce to go with it, adding a couple of spoonfuls of Madeira and some white wine. At Saint-Jean-de-Côle, they grill such cuts of meat and serve them with redcurrants to add a piquancy. You can find this dish, too, served in Piégut-Pluviers, many miles away. It may also be served with a *sauce périgueux*, or, if it has been fried, with a reduced sauce made from a glass of white wine, a tablespoonful of cognac and a cup of *bouillon* added to the pan and then simmered to achieve a *jus* of the right consistency. This is often served with a *steak au poivre*.

Other gastronomic regions of the world might despise the equal care taken over something as apparently insignificant as a potato. But once you have sampled the different skills with which Dordogne cooks cope with this vegetable, you begin to despise such gastronomic *hauteur*. Speaking for myself, *pommes sarladaises* is the most refined way of cooking a potato known to mankind. Others might prefer the little balls of potato known as *pommes beynaçoises*, cooked at nearby Beynac-et-Cazenac. Still others prefer *pommes segonzac*, from Périgord *blanc*, where the potato is enhanced with chicken liver, sausage meat and truffles. Equally acceptable is the traditional Dordogne stew made from potatoes and small *champignons*, the purée of potatoes that customarily accompanies *entrecôte*, or potato croquettes with chopped walnuts.

A *salade verte* also holds surprises. At Quinsac they serve you a *salade* made in their traditional way: walnuts, peppers and bacon, as well as the expected lettuce. *Salade périgourdine* uses *frisée* (curly endive) with a piece of toast rubbed with garlic sitting at the bottom of the bowl. Sometimes a dressing will be made with fruity olive oil, at other times walnut, or hazelnut, oil.

One of the most famous meat dishes of this region is an *enchaud périgourdin* – a loin of pork boned, rolled and roasted. You can never be sure exactly which of several ways it will have been prepared.

To cook **Filet de porc enchaud**, as it is prepared in Domme, chop into small pieces six cloves of garlic. Pierce holes into the flesh of a large fillet of pork and insert the pieces of garlic. Salt and pepper the fillet. Pour one large cup of stock into a casserole, and place into it two pigs' feet which have had the bones removed and have been chopped. Add to this some *bouquet garni*. Add the fillet of pork. Cover the casserole and place it into the oven at a moderate heat for about four hours. From time to time add a little water, if necessary.

Remove the pork and place it into a serving dish. Remove the pigs' feet and *bouquet garni*. Pour the remaining sauce over the pork, leave it for 24 hours. Warm up before eating. The pigs' feet can be eaten separately, either with a vinaigrette or grilled.

In Bergerac, the same dish is prepared in a different way which tends to bring out the garlic flavour.

Flatten a large fillet of pork. Smear the flesh with crushed garlic and season with salt and pepper. Roll the fillet and tie it with string, leaving it then to chill for 24 hours. Place the fillet in a casserole, with a large spoonful of goose fat. Mix in a glass of tepid water, salt and pepper. Cover and cook for two hours on a low heat. Serve it on a warm plate.

Here they serve this dish with roast potatoes. And as a variation they serve it cold, surrounded by its gelled juice. The name of the dish probably originated, in fact, from *au chaud* – a general description of the meat served warm.

In my view the gastronomic capital of the Dordogne is not Périgueux but Sarlat, the centre of the area known as the Périgord *noir*. This is the region *par excellence* of the truffle, and the most characteristic dishes use its flavour perfectly. The food is also often extremely rich. Take, for instance, a stuffed fillet of beef *à la Sarladaise*, as proposed by the great Curnonsky. The dish could not be simpler, nor more fattening.

For a **Filet de boeuf à la sarladaise** weighing a kilo, remove the fat from the beef. Incise the fillet from end to end. Stuff inside a mixture made from 225 grammes of *foie gras*, one diced truffle, salt and pepper. Tie the fillet with string and roast for fifty minutes or so, at a heat of 350°F.

Another rich dish from Sarlat is made from the humble potato.

To make **Pommes de terre sautées à la sarladaise** for four persons, you need a kilo of potatoes, half a glass of goose fat, a tablespoon of finely sliced truffles, and salt and pepper. Peel the potatoes and cut them into slices. Wash them carefully and dry them. In a deep frying pan, heat the goose fat. As soon as it is hot, put in the potatoes, seasoning them with salt and pepper. Fry them quickly at first; then reduce the heat. Half cook the potatoes, add the truffles and continue cooking. When the potatoes are cooked, put them into a warm dish and serve immediately.

No-one quite knows whether the Périgord *noir* takes its name from the leaves of the oak forests glowing black as the evening approaches, the truffle – the so-called 'black diamond' of Périgord –

or the dark history of a region where evil ruffians battled for and
cruelly dominated the country from its many châteaux. Certainly it
is an area that still stands slightly apart. The patois, for example,
differs from that elsewhere in Périgord: the word *pech*, for instance,
used for the steep knolls that rise here, often unexpectedly, is found
rarely elsewhere in the Dordogne. For many years a friend who has
owned a house on such a knoll, named and signposted '*Pech de
Giraux*', has frequently had people from elsewhere in the Dordogne
misunderstand and knock on the door seeking the place to fish
(*pêcher*).

The countryside varies widely, including the rich alluvial plains
of the Rivers Vézère and Dordogne, and stretching south to include
Belvès and its forest. The novelist Albéric Cahuet captured the
extraordinary variety of beauty in a description of a sunset on the
river.

'When the sun is setting, you should contemplate the lovely curve of this
river, as it cradles one of the most beautiful countrysides of the whole
world. On the right the rocks could be those of Greece; to the west,
perched high on its hill, Castelnaud resembles a château of the Rhine.
Opposite us bristles a clump of oaks. On the other side of the river is the
sweetness of the French landscape and the richness of our Dordogne
walnuts, while a centuries-old church speaks of the history of this earth,
this water and this sky.'

The landscape of the Dordogne valley itself is very lush, the
countryside rich and green. You enter Périgord *noir* just after
Souillac, pass through Cazoulès and the semi-deserted village of
Millac, then Peyrillac – these sharp-sounding 'ac' suffixes indicating
villages that were founded by the Romans unless they existed even
earlier and the Romans changed their names. Archaeologists have
revealed the remains of Roman legions at Sainte-Nathalène, at
Calviac, at Carsac and at Saint-Vincent-le-Paluel – all hamlets close
by our route which clearly flourished till the late middle ages since
when nothing seems to have changed.

In places the river cuts deep gorges, even though it meanders
slowly. Elsewhere the ground rises as high as 300 metres. On one
such rocky high point is the *bastide* town of Domme. From its great
parapet, or *barre* as the French call it, unfolds a superb view. Sheila
Steen visited the town in 1949, and described that view perfectly.

'Far below the circular fortifications . . . the Dordogne snaked grandly through avenues of poplars dividing an extensive patchwork of fields, sainfoin, silver clover and golden wheat, light-green maize and dark-green tobacco, hachured with light and shadow.'

From Domme, the river flows past the extraordinary village of La Roque-Gageac (where Albéric Cahuet wrote his description of the river). Its narrow streets lead high up into the cliffs and its houses are built into the towering ochre-coloured rock – a dangerous practice, since from time to time some of the rock falls, crushing one, or several, citizens to death. La Roque-Gageac is only a short drive from château Beynac, once the stronghold of the French in desperate conflict with the English, and château de Castelnaud, bastion of the English. The two strongholds still fiercely glare at each other across the peaceful river. This is the home of *pommes de terre beynaçoises*, round, puffed-up crispy balls of potato. Another local way of serving potatoes is in a *ragoût*. For this firm potatoes are best.

🔥

To cook **Ragoût de pommes de terre aux champignons** you need 450 grammes of potatoes, cut into pieces, a clove of chopped garlic, three skinned and pipped tomatoes, some chopped shallots and two chopped onions, as well as a dozen pieces of *champignon*. Lightly fry the shallots, garlic and onions in a casserole in goose fat. Add the potatoes and let them cook a little without browning. Add hot water to cover the vegetables, and then add the mushrooms and the tomatoes. Boil till the potatoes are cooked.

The valley of the Vézère is the second great river valley of Périgord *noir*. Unusually, much of the agriculture here is taken up with large plantations, profiting from the alluvial plains created by this glistening, meandering river. Even so, less than 40% of the valley is cultivated land. Part of the grandeur of the landscape derives from its steep, rocky slopes, which are too precipitous to plough. Over half the valley is thick with oaks and chestnut trees. And it is flanked all along by countless secondary residences built in the glowing local stone.

Two-thirds of the cultivated land in this valley is devoted to raising cattle food: grass and maize in particular. The farmers' chief revenue here comes from milk – Dordogne farmers supply some 3 million hectolitres a year. Between 1955 and 1970 the number of cows grazing here doubled to 35,000, most of them extremely productive black and white friesians. During the same period the farmers of the Vézère valley seem to have abandoned the notion of selling wine. Vines disappeared, apart from the few needed to supply the farmer and his own family. Increasingly, more profitable walnut trees, planted in irregular rows, replaced them and enhanced the breathtaking beauty of the countryside as well as the farmer's annual income. And around Aubas and Limeuil there are comparatively new high alluvial terraces of fruit trees – apples, plums, peaches – covering over 150 hectares of land, at least twice as much as thirty years ago. Maize and walnuts, vetch and poplars, geese and sheep all combine to create an irresistible landscape.

One of the most typical country dishes, though by no means unique to this region, *navarin de mouton* is a *ragoût* enriched by an assortment of vegetables and herbs varied according to availability.

To cook **Navarin de mouton** for four people you need a kilo of shoulder of mutton, boned and cut into pieces; half a teacup of oil; 50 grammes of goose fat; 600 ml of stock; twenty small onions; eight small carrots; four small turnips; 150 grammes of small peas; 150 grammes of green beans; an onion pierced with cloves; sprigs of fresh rosemary; finely chopped parsley; a soupspoonful of flour; salt and pepper. Heat the oil in a stewing pan and put in the goose fat. When melted, add to the pan the pieces of mutton and the onions. Let the dish cook gently till lightly browned and then sprinkle in the flour. Mix together, again gently, till the flour begins to brown. Now add the stock and then the onion with its cloves. Salt and pepper and add the herbs. Add the carrots and turnips. Wash the green beans and cut them into smallish pieces (usually I have seen people simply cut them in half). Blanche for five minutes in hot salted water. Strain and add to the stewing pan, along with the peas. Cook

gently for 1½ hours. Just before serving, sprinkle some
finely chopped parsley on to the dish.

The sauce and vegetables in a *navarin* are never quite the same.
Sometimes potatoes are added, or used instead of the turnips, and
any of the vegetables out of season may well be omitted. Chopped
tomatoes may also be added to the sauce.

Another excellent dish is made from sheep's tongues. Allow two
per person.

&

For **Langues de mouton braisées** soak the tongues and
blanche them. Next skin them, and add seasoning. Take
strips of fatty bacon and lay them across the tongues. Put
them to cook in a pot on top of a little grated fat. For
more seasoning add an onion, a few pieces of carrot, a
fragment of bay leaf, and some diced pieces of fat. Begin
to cook, and as the fat melts add stock, reducing the heat
and continuing to simmer for 45 minutes to 1 hour.
When the tongues are cooked *au point*, serve them,
garnishing either with a piquant sauce or dressing.

It is easy to see how the Ribéraçois in the eastern region of the
département is dubbed Périgord *blanc*. Chalky strata of rocks provide
the white stones for its houses and farms. The countryside in this
part of the Dronne valley is less lush and the superabundance of
game and fowl is less obvious than farther west. Some have gone so
far as to declare its rocky outcrops boring, monotonous. I agree
with the words Eugène Le Roy put into the mouth of Jacquou le
Croquant.

'I love those grassy valleys, brushed by the snouts of wild boars; those
rocky plateaux strewn with pink heather and broom and golden flowering
gorse; those vast stretches of tall heather – refuges for the hunted beasts;
those little clearings on the tops of the ridges, where the thin soil is thick
with lavender, thyme, everlasting wild thyme, sweet marjoram, whose
perfume rose to my nostrils as I strode by.'

Around Ribérac are pine woods planted in the late nineteenth and
early twentieth centuries. I have never seen much use being made of

these woods, but one of the delights of visiting the town's Wednesday markets consists of handling and buying the wicker-work baskets and furniture made traditionally in these parts.

Ribérac is also renowned for its white calves. On the menu of our local restaurants the cheap unglamorous shin of veal will probably appear as *jarret de veau aux olives*. Essentially you will be served the same dish as appears at meals in ordinary homes throughout the Dordogne.

☙

To cook **Jarret de veau aux olives** for four people you need one shin of veal (weighing about a kilo) cut into pieces, six tomatoes, five onions, two cloves of garlic, a soupspoonful of flour, a glass of dry white wine, 150 grammes of green olives, a *bouquet garni*, 75 grammes of goose fat, salt and pepper. Chop the onions finely. Place the tomatoes in boiling water and then skin them. Peel the cloves of garlic. Season the shin of veal and roll in the flour. Place the goose fat in a casserole and melt until it begins to bubble. Put in the pieces of veal and cook gently until browned all over – about five minutes will be long enough. Place the onions, garlic, tomatoes and *bouquet garni* into the casserole and mix well. Pour the wine over the meat and add half a glass of water. Season. Cover the casserole and cook gently for 1½ hours. Thirty minutes before the end of the cooking, add the green olives to a pan of cold water. Heat the water, and when it begins to boil remove the olives. Drain. Add them to the meat, allowing them to cook with the meat for the final ten minutes. Serve hot.

Ris de veau, calves' sweetbreads, are considered a great delicacy. Although they may often be listed on a menu only as *ris de veau* they may arrive served in a number of different ways. Quite often they are with a *sauce périgueux*. More unusually, I once ate them *au gratin*, in a *béchamel* sauce on a bed of spinach.

☙

For **Ris de veau au gratin** soak the sweetbreads in cold water for several hours. Scald over heat until they boil.

Cool and drain. Cut the sweetbreads into thick slices.
Salt and pepper. Sauté them in butter or goose fat. Make
a *béchamel* sauce. Scald spinach and put on a serving dish.
Add the sweetbreads. Cover with the *béchamel* sauce; add
grated cheese and brown in the oven.

I once ate tripe, *gras-double*, in Ribérac, cooked in a quite astounding
fashion. I do not like this repellent piece of offal, but in fairness I
should give the recipe, for those who do have the taste for it.
Certainly it has far more in its favour gastronomically than the tripe
and onions tucked into by many of our countrymen.

To cook **Tripe à la mode de Ribérac** for six persons
you need 1½ kilos of tripe (*gras-double*), two leeks, three
onions, half a glass of oil, the juice of a lemon, half a
bottle of Bergerac *blanc sec*, a tablespoonful of flour,
bouquet garni, four cloves of garlic, basil, two egg yolks,
parsley, salt and pepper. You cut the tripe into strips and
slice up the leeks; peel the onions and cut them in two;
flatten the garlic. Put the onions and the leeks into half a
glass of oil in a pan, and heat. As soon as they begin to
yellow, reduce the heat and add the flour, mixing with a
wooden spoon, thinning with the white wine and a litre
of boiling water. Add the tripe and the garlic, the *bouquet
garni* and half the lemon juice. Simmer very very gently
for four hours. Crush a little more garlic with the basil,
slowly adding two spoonfuls of oil until you have a fine
paste. Mix with this the two egg yolks, watering it down
with a ladle full of the *bouillon* from the tripe. Pour this
over the tripe, stirring continuously and not allowing it
to come to the boil. Add the rest of the lemon juice,
sprinkle with parsley, and serve very hot.

I am sorry not to have enjoyed a dish that took four hours to
prepare, and I have thought subsequently that the recipe could
easily be adapted for a *ragoût de veau* or fish stew. It is close to
bordelais recipes in its use of leeks and wine, but the basil paste is
unusual.

By contrast with the Ribérac area the region around Bergerac is so warm and gentle that some people in Périgord instinctively separate the two. Hills and slopes and little valleys converging on to the rivers cohere in one agreeable, unhurried countryside. The skies are bluer, the weather is warm and dry. This is wine country – best seen, incidentally, from the little train that trundles back and forth from Sarlat to Bordeaux. This is also tobacco country; in fact it is now produced in greater quantities outside the Dordogne only in Lot-et-Garonne. Initially, tobacco planting spread slowly here after Bonaparte's state monopoly was finally lifted in 1859. By 1863, the *arrondissement* of Sarlat, for example, produced tobacco on only ninety hectares of its fertile land. But as the profitability of the crops increased, so did demands that the importing of Virginia tobacco be banned and in 1910 the first congress of tobacco planters held at Bergerac was attended by no fewer than 700 participants. Needless to say, most of them sat down to an immense banquet.

The brown, powerful cigarettes that hang from the lips of many a chain-smoking Frenchman are now being replaced by *tabac blond*, the yellow-white tobacco said to be far less harmful to a person's health. Whatever the gain in smokers' health, many producers regret this new technique, for the simple reason that the processing – drying the plants in large ovens for only five or six days – creates far less work. One of my friends comes from a family that has produced tobacco for several generations. He tells me how much he resents working in one of the Sarlat supermarkets, since the production of *tabac blond* has made him redundant at home. He also predicts – gloomily – that what he calls 'scaremongers' are contributing to the decline of an industry worth 120 million francs a year to this one *département* of France. Looking anxiously to the future, a number of tobacco farmers have already begun replacing the crop with strawberries.

Périgord *blanc* also for a long time boasted – if that is the word – the gloomy, dangerous forest of la Double, set between the rivers Dronne, Isle and Beauronne. Like the other forests of the region, it was for centuries the haunt of criminals, fugitives, the very poor, madmen and wild animals. One essential worker lived his miserable life here, namely the charcoal-burner, but improved transport bringing supplies of coke for fuel put him out of business. In the eighteenth century some enlightened monks and *intendents* attempted to construct roads through the la Double forest. Swamps were drained and the soil was improved. Several artificial lakes were created and stocked with fish. Soon, however, all was neglected again. 'The lakes,' observed Eugène Le Roy, 'exude only pestilential odours, which creep over all this savage, solitary part of the land.' In addition the canalisation of the River Isle made it profitable to sell the wood of this forest in other regions. The trade was exploited ruthlessly. Much of the forest was transformed into gorse-land: bogs and swamps returned.

Today the forest still exudes an air of solitude, and the woodland has kept its beauty. 'I loved the forest, in spite of its evil reputation,' Jacquou le Croquant muses at one point. 'I loved those tremendous masses of woods that followed the rises of ground, covering the country with a green cloak in summer, turning into every colour in autumn – yellows, pale greens, russets, browns – according to the species of the trees, and pierced here and there by the bright red of wild cherry trees or the dark green of some scattered clumps of pine.' The traditional industries linked to the forest have also survived: furniture, paper, building, cellulose and the tanneries of Périgueux, Bergerac and Sarlat still depend in some measure on the forest.

Apart from pine trees, the forests are made up chiefly of oaks – of many kinds – and of great chestnut trees. The fruit of these trees has become a culinary delicacy in the Dordogne. Today, they are increasingly grown for *marrons glacés*, but this is largely for export. Within the region they are more commonly called *châtaignes*. As in Britain, people roast them on the open fire. But here, they were once a staple food – boiled and braised to be eaten with meat and particularly game, like potatoes. These *châtaignes blanchies* are an ancient Dordogne recipe, steaming the sweet chestnuts over potatoes before serving them in a number of ways.

🔥

Take a kilo of chestnuts for **Châtaignes blanchies**. Take off their outer skins with a sharp knife. Put them in lightly boiling water to which you have added a little salt, covering the pot. After ten minutes or so you should be able to remove the second skin quite easily, without damaging the pulp. Remove the second skin from each chestnut, and wash them all in clean water. To stop the chestnuts sticking to the base of the pot while they are cooking, place them on a layer of potatoes. The aim is to cook the chestnuts in steam, so pour only a little water in the pot, before bringing the pot to the heat. Steam until tender.

The regional variations of this ancient Dordogne recipe are legion. Instead of placing them on a layer of potatoes while cooking, some will wrap the skinned chestnuts in cabbage leaves, sewing these into a bag – and incidentally giving a slightly different flavour to the dish. Today, when chestnuts served with meat or game are usually braised in stock, it is the custom to drench these chestnuts in sweet white wine before eating them. Other parts of the Dordogne add butter before eating them.

The Périgord *vert* in the northernmost parts of Périgord, is better known as the Nontronnais, from its chief town, Nontron, and acquired its name far more recently than either Périgord *noir* or *blanc*. The green, obviously, describes the lushness of the landscape, which is akin to that of neighbouring Limousin.

The terrain, mostly formed of granite or of fine-grained schistose rocks formed by great heat and pressure long ago, gives rough country compared with other parts of the Dordogne, and at times its rivers – the upper Dronne, the Bandiat, the upper Isle and the Auvézère – break into highly impressive gorges. In the nineteenth century the force of these tumbling rivers drove iron forges renowned throughout France. As the century wore on the British, in particular, developed better methods of producing iron and steel. For a time the hundred forges of this region were protected by import taxes on foreign metal; but when Napoleon III abolished these, the industry went into decline. Not a single forge works in this region today.

The charm of the Nontronnais lies in its small towns, little villages, farms that are either isolated or grouped into hamlets. Many of these farms have huge barns which served to store such grain as could be saved and also to house pigs, rabbits and cows. Some of the hamlets and villages are exquisite. To the east of the region vegetables, fruit trees and walnuts have made a fair number of farmers quite rich, though I have never found one to admit it.

Walnuts, in particular, are big business and Terrasson, where the River Vézère enters Périgord, has grown especially rich and contented on them. Every Thursday a thriving walnut market, the largest in the region, is held there. An old town with an ancient, twelfth-century bridge, it gives the sense of bursting at the seams since its population has nearly doubled in the past two decades.

One of the famous sons of Périgord *vert* is General Bugeaud, who conquered Algeria for the French and erected there a huge statue in his own honour. When the Algerians gained their independence, they showed what they thought of Bugeaud by sending the statue back. You can see it today at Excideuil, his home village. But Bugeaud was also an influential and inventive farmer. In the first half of the nineteenth century he used the fortune he had amassed as a soldier to introduce better grasses into his domaines. This did not make him popular, since he steadfastly refused to increase what he allowed his tenant-farmers to earn. He found they clung to old methods of farming, in spite of his own innovations. Even so, Bugeaud's reforms greatly increased the head of cattle supported by the pastures around Excideuil, thus indirectly ameliorating the lot of the peasant farmers as well. Quite simply, whatever people thought of General Bugeaud personally, because of his reforms there was more to eat.

The new grasses introduced by Bugeaud and like-minded reformers still support the large cattle of this region, which provide most of the beef of the Dordogne. Fields full of heifers surround farms which produce butter and white calves for the butcher. Close by Sarrazac, near Excideuil, I so much enjoyed a delicious, simply braised veal dish that I found the recipe. Not entirely dissimilar from an *enchaud*, it has a light, fresh tomato sauce to moisten the dryer cut of meat used.

❦

For a **Fricandeau de Nontron** take a piece of fillet of veal weighing about 1¼ kilos. Pierce the flesh with a sharp pointed knife and insert slivers of garlic. Rub all over with salt and pepper, and brown the meat in olive oil. Turn the heat down, and add twelve whole tomatoes, twelve small onions, two chopped shallots, a sprig of

rosemary and seasoning to taste. Cover the pan and cook
very gently without any water. If the pan should get dry,
add a little stock. When the veal is cooked, serve it on a
bed of onions, with the tomatoes around it.

Another good veal dish from Périgord *vert* are *côtelettes nontron-
naises*, served thickly sprinkled with breadcrumbs fried with garlic
and parsley.

Apart from the beef dishes you would expect to find everywhere
– *daubes, entrecôtes, steaks au poivre* and *boeuf à la mode* – you will also
find excellent local ways of preparing the cheaper cuts and offal.
Here is a very good way in which they cook *langue de boeuf*.

Freshen the tongue for **Langue de boeuf** by first
scrubbing it under warm water and then letting it soak in
cold water for two to three hours. Drain and dry it.
Before cooking, the tongue should be salted to improve
the flavour. Place it in a casserole just big enough to hold
it, after spreading about ¼ inch layer of coarse salt on the
bottom. Then cover the tongue with another ¼ inch layer
of salt and place wax paper on top. Weight it down with a
plate and leave in a refrigerator overnight. When you are
ready to cook, wash off the salt. Simmer the tongue for
two hours and then peel off its skin. Pre-heat the oven to
350°F. In a casserole cook in *lardons* and oil 225 grammes
of sliced carrots and 225 grammes of sliced onions, along
with 150 grammes of diced boiled ham. Cook this over a
moderately low heat, stirring frequently, until the vegetables are tender. Salt and pepper the tongue and place in
the casserole. Turn it and baste it with the vegetables and
the oil. Cover the casserole, and leave the tongue for ten
minutes. Turn the tongue and baste again and leave for
another ten minutes. Pour into the casserole four tablespoonfuls of Madeira and 125 ml of white wine. Boil
down rapidly. Add also one whole tomato, roughly
chopped, one large clove of garlic, one bay leaf, half a
teaspoonful of thyme; pour in enough stock to come
two-thirds of the way up the tongue. Bring the liquid in
the casserole to a gentle simmer. Cover the casserole and

put it low down in the pre-heated oven. After thirty minutes check to see that the liquid in the casserole is simmering slowly and steadily. Once again baste the tongue. Turn the thermostat down to 325°F, and when the tongue has braised for another hour, turn it onto its other side. The tongue should be fully cooked in two-and-a-half hours.

Some people regard offal and variety meats as inferior or distasteful – but I regard the ability to transform these and appreciate them as delicacies as the mark of a first-rate cook. Here, the chefs of Périgord excel and the regional variety shows itself very clearly. At Neuvic you will be teased with the *confit de porc*; at Bouzic try the *tortières de gésiers d'oie* (goose-gizzard pies); at Mauzac the restaurant 'La Métairie' suggests to its guests *ris de veau aux morilles*; at Badefols-sur-Dordogne the chef's speciality is *foie gras maison*; at Brantôme the restaurant called 'Le Moulin de L'Abbaye' will offer you goose-gizzard salad – and each is offered with the same pride as the most expensive dish on the menu.

The Wines of the Dordogne

'God made water, but man made wine.'

VICTOR HUGO

We scarcely ever drink wine from a supermarket or shop when visiting our neighbours. We are invariably offered instead wine made by themselves from grapes they have cultivated. It is offered, rightly, with a certain pride. We are always informed that this is simple, pure, fresh wine. 'There's no chemical nonsense in this bottle', the farmer's wife will proclaim. Dark hints are dropped about the bizarre additives in wine you might buy elsewhere: chemical preservatives, too much sugar, vegetable juice. That sort of additive does not only produce bad wine, we are warned; it is also bad for your health.

I like to imagine the possible variations on this conversation. Throughout the whole region wine lovers are fond of quoting a certain Professor Besançon of Bergerac, who used to say, 'To drink water you have to be mad. Water never cemented friendships. And water is always contaminated, always dirty. There is really no such thing as water that is fit to drink.' Often, of course, a conversation will take place in gestures as well as words. None are more eloquent than those connected with wine. A farmer will indicate that he has a little more *eau-de-vie* stashed away than people imagine; as he does so, he gestures behind his back with his right hand. Offering one of his own wines, he will indicate its excellence by extending his right hand, thumb upwards. As he suggests that *eau-de-vie* might, perhaps, go to one's head, he proffers an extraordinary gesture, as if he was twisting off the end of his nose.

You receive more solemn advice when you buy wine from one of the *caves-coopératives* in Périgord. 'Don't forget that this wine is a living thing. If you are going to move it around, you have to let it lie still again for a fortnight. Before drinking it, leave it in the dining-room for twenty-four hours; and open the bottle two or three hours before you need to start drinking.' For the very fine wines of this region, say an expensive Pécharmant, the *vigneron* is absolutely right. Great care has gone into making these wines and they deserve respect. Care should be taken in drinking them.

Every wine-growing region of France boasts a group of wine-lovers dedicated to maintaining and, if possible, improving the standards of their own *vignerons*, to electing officers and to honouring local lovers of the grape. Here, in Périgord, that group are the *consuls de la vinée* of Bergerac, whose home is the wine museum there. Here the cult of divine liquor is celebrated with pomp and gravity, with ritual tastings and annual processions, with thanksgivings for fine vintages and anxious speeches over lesser ones.

Sometimes the chapter of the Wine Consuls welcomes new members. There is great excitement as people wait outside the cloister. Suddenly the heavy door is flung open. Those privileged to enter file inside, passing through the magnificent galleries of the sixteenth and seventeenth centuries to the ancient chamber where the ceremony will take place. The six consuls, dressed in their red and gold robes and toque hats, address the candidates for admission to the order. In truth they are apostrophizing the wines of the Dordogne:

'Lovers of wine, let us exalt together the rich vintages of Périgord, and above all the fruits of our own locality: the shimmering *blancs secs* and *rosés* of Bergerac and of Montravel, so agreeable with our trout; the full-bodied reds of Bergerac and Pécharmant, which admirably expand the flavours of the meats of our region; the *blancs moelleux* of Rosette, Côtes de Bergerac and Montravel, along with those of Saussignac, which Rabelais loved, and, above all, those of Monbazillac, which add such dignity to a *foie gras* well-seasoned with our Dordogne truffle.'

Another consul declares himself certain that the candidates for admission to the order will be worthy ambassadors of these wines. Another bids them prudently not to waste their time drinking water, 'an insipid and colourless liquid, which inspires melancholy and creates bad complexions'. So the ceremony continues until, finally, everyone swears – in the presence of notaries – to uphold the cause of Périgord wines, and the candidates' signatures are written in the books of the order. I often wonder how many of the elected Consuls surreptitiously buy the wines of other regions now so widely available in shops and supermarkets.

The peoples of Périgord have been making wine for a very long time, certainly as far back as Roman-Gaulish times. At the beginning of the Christian era the poet Ausonius sang the praises of Dordogne wines. During the Hundred Years' War the English took a particular delight in them: the chronicler Froissart records that on the eve of the battle for Bergerac in 1345 the troops of the Earl of Derby passed the night very happily drinking a large quantity of the excellent local wines, which cost them next to nothing. No doubt it was this experience which inspired them to take the town, and the Earl to become its lord. Thenceforth wines from around Bergerac were taken by river as far as Libourne, or Blaye, before being dispatched by sea to England. The battle of Castillon in 1453 liberated south-west France from the English and for a time stopped this profitable trade, beer replacing wine as the staple British drink, but the trade revived again during the course of the fifteenth century.

Naturally people quarrelled over the wine trade. Many *vignerons* whose vineyards lay to the south-west of Périgord greatly disliked the river traffic which brought downstream rival wines, and they frequently tried, by foul means as well as fair, to stop it. Invariably they failed. They also fought against the royal exchequer. In the sixteenth century vineyards planted on the right, or north, bank of the Dordogne had greater duties levied on them than those on the left bank. Sometimes the *bourgeoisie* of Ribérac were required to hand over their finest *crus*. In consequence, many transplanted their vines to the south bank where the taxes, not to speak also of the weather, were more clement. Disputes about the boundaries of each *vigneron's* parcels of land were, in consequence, legion, and the limits are still jealously guarded today.

Bergerac wines in particular were valued abroad, being increasingly exported to Ireland, Scandinavia, Scotland and Holland as time passed. As a Protestant stronghold, the town lost many citizens to the Netherlands when Louis XIV revoked the Edict of Nantes in 1685 and began to persecute the Huguenots. These religious fugitives did not lose their taste for wine, which, as the Bible observed, was created to make glad the heart of man, and the link considerably boosted the export of Bergerac wine there.

At the beginning of the nineteenth century red wine from Bergerac was reputed to keep well for anything from three to thirty years and much was exported, though it then lost its name and simply was known as claret from south-west France. An exception was the fine wine produced in the commune of Saint-Léon-sur-Vézère, which was transported to Bergerac and exported without becoming anonymous. The average yearly wine-production of the whole *département* in these prospering years was around 603,500 hectolitres, with the Bergerac area producing most: in 1837 165,000 hectolitres.

But other regions of the Dordogne were rich in vineyards too. Sarlat and its region produced 118,000 hectolitres. The Ribéraçois produced 95,000 hectolitres. Around Périgueux 76,000 hectolitres were made; and the Nontronnais produced nearly 56,000 hectolitres. Huge amounts of sweet white wine from Monbazillac were reaching Holland. Wines from around Périgueux lacked fame, save for that from Saint-Pantaly-d'Ans, which Henri IV loved, but were plentiful. Much wine was produced around Sarlat to be drunk locally, though some from Domme was renowned and transported as far as Bordeaux. That made around Terrasson was exported to the mountains of Limousin, to Lower Auvergne and to La Marche, while Ribérac exported its Rossignols as far as Haut-Vienne.

Nothing like the quantities of the early nineteenth century are produced today. The viticulture of the Dordogne was virtually destroyed in the second half of the century by the vine-pest phylloxera, first discovered near Bordeaux in the mid-1860s. A *département* which in 1866 grew vines on 96,000 hectares of land could muster scarcely 31,000 hectares for the same crop by the end of the century. Only in the region around Bergerac have the vineyards of the Dordogne really recovered. Today this region grows vines capable of producing *appellation contrôlée* wines on an area totalling over 100,000 hectares, on average producing annually 250,000 hectolitres of such red and white wines. Another 250,000 hectares of the Dordogne produce wines which do not receive the accolade *appellation contrôlée*, but which should not be despised. Around Domme, around Périgueux and around Nontron such wines are produced for the farmer's personal consumption. Wines from outside the *département* are also plentifully displayed on the shelves of the local stores and supermarkets: Côtes de Duras, for example, a dry white wine grown forty-five kilometres south-west of Bergerac in the *département* of Lot-et-Garonne, is drunk a good deal here.

The quality of wine produced by farmers still varies on an individual basis within the same year due to the element of chance affecting a number of vital factors; these same problems, multiplied and seen within a general perspective, determine whether or not each year is a good, moderate or bad one for the *département* as a whole, and that, in turn, determines the quantity, quality and price of the wines such as are bought by ourselves and our visitors. The outcome cannot be confidently predicted until the *vendange*, or harvest. That comes late, due to the long summers in this region. I have never known my neighbour predict that the vintage will be excellent until it is virtually harvested. Instead he talks about threats to his grapes. Our region is prone to short but unexpectedly savage hail storms, with stones far bigger than any I have encountered in Britain. Everyone insures his roof against them. But you cannot insure your vines in the same way. Once the vintage is damaged, that is that. Vines can survive winter frosts, but later frosts, when vines have begun to shoot again, severely set back essential growth.

Everything went miraculously right for the vines in 1982 and 1983 – the rain, sun, humidity were what everyone prayed for. The prices came down for very pleasing château-bottled reds and whites. Initially 1984 seemed to be following suit. Then the vineyard scourge known as *coulure* appeared, fortunately after many vines had flowered. Those still to flower failed to pollinate. To make matters worse a second scourge, the so-called *miller-andange*, which stops the grapes from developing properly, then affected other vines.

Since no-one can convincingly explain why such scourges appear, or why they affect only certain categories of grape, there is much wine lore concerning the success or failure of the harvest. In 1984 the grape that suffered most was the Merlot variety. One of my neighbours had taken a delivery of Italian vines some years ago and thus escaped the problems. His theory was that too much wine had been produced in the previous couple of years and that the vines were deliberately taking a rest.

Which, then, are the best of the wines of the Dordogne? The red *appellation contrôlée* wines are Pécharmant, Bergerac Supérieur and Bergerac; the white ones are Bergerac Supérieur, Bergerac, Monbazillac-Rosette, Rosette-Monṭravel, Côtes Montravel and Haut-Montravel. The list is constantly checked and revised by a committee of wine-tasters drawn from each commune in the region. The red wines can all be drunk reasonably young. The dry white wines have been fermented at the low temperature of 18°, to keep their fine aromas.

My own favourites are the sweet *liquoreux* Monbazillac, which is so strong that I dare drink no more than a couple of glasses late in the evening, the *aromatique* Bergerac *sec* 'Sauvignon', which makes a lovely *apéritif* drunk quite cold at, say, 8°, and the fruitier Bergerac *sec* 'Blanc de Blancs', to my mind best drunk even colder, as a fine complement to *hors d'oeuvre*, a fish course, or a soft goat's cheese towards the end of the meal. In a good year Rosette, a *moelleux*, or medium-sweet white wine is a very rare treat. The *vignerons* tell you to serve it sharply chilled, between 6° and 8°, and recommend that you drink it with fish, and, more particularly, *entrées* made from the varied mushrooms of the Dordogne, but it is also strong enough to accompany dishes made with truffles.

What I find particularly delightful about the wines of this part of Périgord is their variety, a reflection in part of the continually changing landscape. The soils themselves vary: clay and silica around Bergerac, clay and limestone around Monbazillac, clay, silica and sand at Montravel. The lie of the land also counts. Rosette, for instance, derives its pale straw colour and supple, fruity bouquet from its grape, but also from the sunny slopes and the soil north of Bergerac where the vines grow. Again, the grapes used for Montravel and Bergerac whites are exactly the same: it is the lie of the land of the vineyards and the quality of the soil which make the differences. Since, in fact, Bergerac wines are grown over a comparatively wide area, they display considerable variety for the same reasons. Some vines grow on alluvial silt; other soils are composed of chalk and siliceous clays. Traces of flint add fragrance and sap, say the farmers.

The easiest way to buy wines in Périgord, as elsewhere, is from supermarkets. But the most enchanting way, by which you will learn about the wines as part of the culture of this region, is to visit the vineyards. From Bergerac to Sigoulès, for example, you can visit a Gothic church and see an old windmill before buying good wines from the *cave-coopérative*. Visit château Corbiac in the Pécharmant region where wine grapes have been cultivated for at least five centuries; admire its lawns and gardens as well as its architecture, and then buy its wine.

To visit the Mobazillac vineyards takes at least a day, if you are to explore even half of its delights. Château Monbazillac itself is the home of a Protestant museum, for this once was Huguenot country. Built by the Vicomte de Ribérac in 1550, it has all the ingredients of a model château – turrets, a moat, battlements, crenellations. Now it is owned by the Union de Coopératives de la Dordogne, who are very ready to supply you with as much Monbazillac as you can carry away, and have also provided a car park and restaurant.

The Montravel vineyards spread over fifteen communes on the right bank of the Dordogne, close by the château of Saint-Michel-de-Montaigne. Here, in the sixteenth century, lived the famous essayist and philosopher Michel Eyquem de Montaigne, and from his study window he would look out on vineyards growing then exactly as they do today. You can still visit the château. Of the one Montaigne lived in, only his library remains: a quaint circular tower, inscribed with half-sad texts on the beams to remind men and women of their mortality. Montaigne himself loved the Montravel wines he kept in the cellar of his château, remarking once that 'With this wine the good God gives gaiety to mankind and youth back to old men.' You can pause in the Romanesque church here for a moment, where this gentle Christian's heart is buried.

If you wished, you could also combine the trip with a visit to Montcaret, just on the borders of Bordelais, where a lovely Roman mosaic has been excavated outside a Romanesque church.

Before we bought our house in the Dordogne we even then derived great pleasure from driving round the vineyards in summer, sampling a little wine in the *caves-coopératives* – but not too much for the French police are strict with drunken drivers, talking to the farmers, buying what we fancied. We would also add to the enjoyment by accompanying food in local restaurants with their matching local wines.

These wines are becoming increasingly well-known, some of them even appearing on the shelves of wine-merchants abroad – and justly so, for although they are frequently cheaper than more familiar names, they are often at least as good. Bergerac (both white, red or *rosé*), Montravel wines, and above all Monbazillac and Pécharmant are wines that for me nowadays all carry warm memories of sipping by the fire of an evening or lazing on our terrace on warm autumn afternoons.

From these exploratory trips I learnt three valuable things. First, there are no fixed rules determining which wine accompanies which dish and our British concern for what is 'correct' really ought to be jettisoned. So, for example, the French will often drink a light, fruity red wine with fish, cooling the wine slightly first. Second, the best way of learning how to enhance recipes with a judicious glass of exactly the right wine is from the menus of chefs who have behind them many years of experiment and the advice of home cooks who habitually use it as a local ingredient, rather than books. Third, by coming to realise the quality of the frequently under-estimated wines, I learnt that there are fashions in wines which, like fashions in clothes, can obscure the charm and even the splendour of what is foolishly considered *démodé* or not quite up to scratch.

Of all the wine-labels of Périgord the ones you see most carry the name Bergerac. Sometimes despised by those who ought to know better, or are merely repeating what they have read in other people's books and not what their own palates tell them, the wine-growers of Bergerac have adapted to the times, have overcome disadvantages and poor publicity, and have succeeded in producing wines satisfying to the discriminating as well as to the tyro who simply wants to taste and experiment. In some Dordogne restaurants the *patron* offers to his customers an *appellation contrôlée* red Bergerac as his *vin ordinaire*, often selling it at little more than twice the price on the supermarket shelves. To me this is an amazing bargain. Indeed, there is one really remarkable feature of this viticulture. While most wine-growing regions of France are better known for either red or white *appellation contrôlée* vintages, the *vignerons* of Bergerac achieve both, and at qualities varying from an acceptable wine to a great one. Some *rosé* Bergerac wines are also judged fit to be declared *appellation contrôlée*.

The grapes reserved for the red wines of Bergerac are those also used for red Bordeaux – Cabernet Franc, Cabernet Sauvignon, Malbec and Merlot. As for whites, there are three authorised varieties of grape: Sémellons, Muscadelle and Sauvignon. These produce the excellent Côtes de Bergerac and, south of the river, Côtes de Saussignac – sweet and yet quite gentle too. For dry white wines, 25% of Ugni Blanc may be added, provided the quantity does not exceed that of the Sauvignon grape. For many years far more white, especially *liquoreux*, wines were produced. But in the past twenty years half the *appellation contrôlée* wines of Bergerac have been red. They tell you to drink these red wines young, though the wines with more body can be kept for up to five years, improving all the time. No-one recommends laying down a dry white Bergerac for any length of time, but the sweet whites are said to improve greatly with age.

Since the river is full of pike, shad, salmon and lamprey, the sweet white Bergerac is much in demand locally. Often I have seen people accompany these dishes instead with the rarer, thirst-quenching *rosé* wines that the *vignerons* of Bergerac also produce. 'Monsieur de Bergerac', as the locals call straightforward Bergerac *rouge*, is often drunk throughout a meal in these parts. It is also used extensively in cooking, and not simply because it is good value. A *coq au vin* tastes fine when cooked in *vin ordinaire*, but cooked in Bergerac *rouge* it tastes infinitely better – tangy and without the heaviness sometimes resulting from a fuller wine.

🕯️

For **Coq au Monsieur de Bergerac** you will need a roasting chicken, 75 grammes of goose fat, a dozen small mushrooms and a dozen small onions, a clove of garlic, some diced fat bacon (two slices), *bouquet garni*, a glass of cognac and a bottle of Bergerac rouge. Cut the chicken into pieces, keeping these in their traditional forms – in other words, both sides of the breast, the thighs, drumsticks and wings. Toss the diced bacon in fat in a casserole, adding the chicken until the pieces are nicely browned. Remove the chicken and cook the onions and mushrooms in the casserole. Add the chicken, the garlic cut in pieces, salt and pepper and the *bouquet garni*. Reheat; *flambé* the chicken with the cognac; pour in the Bergerac. Cover and cook for three- quarters of an hour. When the dish is almost ready, sauté a few slices of bread until brown. Take out the *bouquet garni* and serve the chicken, garnished with the bread.

In Sarlat they serve this dish often in the pan in which it has been cooking. It is a filling meal, which should be accompanied with a bottle of red Bergerac Supérieur.

A more surprising, but equally good combination of flavours made locally is red wine and herrings. We persuaded a man who said he hated herrings to try these.

For **Harengs au Bergerac rouge** you need a quarter of a bottle of good red Bergerac wine, eight small herrings, 100 grammes of butter, four shallots, two cloves of garlic, *bouquet garni*, 150 grammes of smoked bacon, two soupspoonfuls of flour, salt and pepper. Clean the herrings. Salt and pepper them and sprinkle with the flour. Melt 60 grammes of the butter in a frying pan and when this is hot, put in the herrings, lowering the heat. Fry for a few minutes on each side. Cut up the bacon into small pieces and dice the shallots. Crush the garlic. In a shallow casserole, melt 30 grammes of the butter and in this cook the shallots and bacon, adding the red wine, the garlic and the *bouquet garni*. On a gentle flame let this stew for twenty minutes. Add the herrings and cook for a further twenty minutes. Make a *roux* with 10 grammes of butter and the flour. With this thicken the sauce in which the herrings are cooking. Continue to cook for a further five minutes. Serve hot.

We ate these accompanied by a dry white Bergerac. I think I should never have ordered a dry white wine to accompany a fish dish cooked in red wine, unless the restaurateur had not insisted that this was absolutely correct. He was right. The white Bergerac and the herrings converted our friend totally. When it comes to cooking as opposed to eating and drinking, a glass of dry white Bergerac, judiciously added when fish is being poached, gives the dish a lovely, brisk (though in no way overpowering) tang.

In wine country you will often find, for example, *filets de sole pochés au Bergerac blanc*. Usually the fillets of sole, rolled up in a dish, are covered with chopped onions, salt and pepper, chopped parsley and the wine, covered and baked. A thickening of butter and flour, and a garnish of prawns is often added.

More distinctive to the region, *foie gras* is sometimes served with a sauce in the southern parts of the *département*.

&

To make **Foie gras en sauce** you need a tablespoonful of goose fat, two sliced carrots, some thyme, parsley, a bay leaf, an onion, a glass of dry white Bergerac, a glass of veal stock, and a dessertspoonful of flour. Melt the fat in a saucepan, and in it fry the carrots and onion, adding the herbs. As soon as the onion starts to turn yellow, sprinkle in the flour. Cook for ten minutes, adding the wine and continually stirring, slowly adding also the stock. Salt and pepper. Reduce to half, strain through a sieve and cook for another ten minutes. Cut the *foie gras* into slices and serve, pouring the sauce over them. The dish can be further enhanced by adding a tablespoonful of Madeira and a finely chopped truffle just before serving.

Bergerac *blanc sec* also complements a piece of venison very well. Beef or lamb may also be cooked in the same way.

&

For **Chevreuil au Bergerac** you need thickish pieces of *chevreuil* for each person and marinading vegetables to fill the dish – chopped carrots, onions, and a shallot, spiced with garlic. The vegetables should be below the *chevreuil* as well as above it. Pour into this dish not quite a cupful of olive oil and half a bottle of dry white Bergerac. Then let the meat marinate for two days, occasionally stirring it and turning it over. After two days, transfer it all to a casserole. Boil, then lower the heat and let the whole simmer for three hours with the casserole covered. Take out the pieces of *chevreuil* and keep them hot. Sieve the vegetables, put them back into the casserole, heat the sauce and pour it over the *chevreuil*. Serve.

You can cook a pheasant with sweet white Bergerac; use a full glass as the marinade and braising liquid along with half a glass of cognac and half a glass of Madeira. The wines and cognac blend even better used in exactly the same combination in a terrine.

🔥

In order to cook a **Terrine de faisan** embodying one bird you need also fresh chives, sprigs of tarragon and parsley, two cloves of garlic, a small tin of *foie gras*, a truffle and 450 grammes of fat pork. Chop up the herbs and add them to the cognac, Madeira and white wine. Marinate in this liquid the meat of the pheasant, cut into pieces, for twenty-four hours. With the entrails and liver of the bird, plus the pork, make a forcemeat. Season. Coat the inside of a terrine with goose fat. Layer it in turn with the forcemeat, pieces of pheasant, *foie gras*, and very thinly sliced truffle. Finish off with forcemeat. Add the juice of the marinade. Cover and cook at 325°F for an hour and a half. Serve cold.

Madeira appears in many other Dordogne recipes due to its valuable powers of reviving dried truffles.

Of the other wines of the region, let us take first those called Montravel, Haut-Montravel and Côtes de Montravel. The grapes for white Montravel are exactly the same as those used for Bergerac: Sémillon, Sauvignon and Muscadelle. Again, too, for the dry white the *vigneron* may add up to a quarter of the Ugni Blanc grape, provided always that this acid variety in no way swamps the

Sauvignon. The right proportion enhances the bouquet brought by the Sauvignon. The latter two wines, sweet enough to be called *liquoreux* on their labels, mature elegantly and are best drunk four, five or even more years after the vintage. Dry Montravel, on the other hand should be drunk within eighteen months of the harvest, served, they say, at between 8° and 10°.

A not too expensive dry Montravel adds subtlety to the Dordogne version of *sole au vin blanc*, which also uses goose fat.

For **Sole au Montravel** you need eight fillets of sole, salt and pepper, a tablespoon of goose fat, half a bottle of Montravel, and a dessertspoonful of flour. Lay the fillets of sole in a greased fireproof dish. Season, and cook in an oven at 350°F for about twenty-five minutes, covering the dish with greaseproof paper. Take out the fillets, keeping them warm. Reduce the wine in a saucepan, adding flour that has been worked into half a tablespoonful of goose fat. Add *noisettes* of goose fat till you have put in a full tablespoon. Pour this sauce over the fillets and grill the whole dish for a minute.

To my mind, there are two great wines of the Dordogne region: the full red Pécharmant and the sweet white Monbazillac. Pécharmant – deriving from *Péch charmant*, that is 'delightful little hill' – is cultivated on no more than 425 acres of gravelly land from the same four grapes used for Bergerac: Cabernet Franc, Cabernet Sauvignon, Merlot and Malbec. They grow on slopes that contain traces of iron and fine clays, as well as gravel, and when drinking a glass in one of my favourite local restaurants I am *invariably* asked by the proprietor whether I can taste the unique tang of the earth of these 425 acres. I actually believe that I can. Very many *vignerons* still pick the grapes by hand, carefully placing them in a circular tumbril set between the rows of vines and throwing away any cracked fruit.

Although the Malbec grape is said to dominate Pécharmant, undoubtedly the Cabernet Sauvignon – a small red grape that produces a wine containing lots of tannin but able to mature for up to thirty years or even more – is equally important. In its early years

Cabernet Sauvignon carries in its juice a flavour hinting at blackcurrant, but the maturing wine soon loses this, and takes on instead some of the savour of cedarwood. The Merlot is a softer variety and adds its fruitiness, as does the Cabernet Franc. Pécharmant is a powerful wine, very generous and a superb ruby-red in colour. It needs to mature, preferably for five years or more, and is served at about 17°, according to the experts. If you ask a restaurateur what he recommends to accompany Pécharmant, he is likely to suggest a *lièvre à la royale*, or some game, such as a woodcock (*une bécasse*) or a wood pigeon (*une palombe*). Woodcocks are often served roasted, with a rich stuffing made from their own livers and kidneys mixed with sorrel and served with a sauce enriched by a little cognac. Only a red wine with the body and roundness of a Pécharmant can cope with such a dish.

🔥

> For such a **Bécasse rôtie**, served with croûtons, cover the plucked and cleaned woodcock with fat bacon strips and roast it rare. The entrails and the livers are chopped and garnished with sorrel and lemon juice, mashed into a purée, which is spread on the croûtons. Take the juice from the roasting tin and deglaze it with cognac. Add some game stock, and then reduce. Traditionally the sauce would be thickened with a purée of goose-liver before pouring over the woodcock.

Similarly, *boeuf au Pécharmant* is a powerful dish. The French do not consider it a waste when good wine is used for cooking. Essentially this is a superior *boeuf à la mode* such as is found in many other regions of France as well. Nevertheless, it subtly changes in character if the wine involved happens to be good Pécharmant. This is a dish that takes time and care, but it is hard to imagine time and care spent for a better purpose. Buy the topside of the beef.

🔥

> For **Boeuf au Pécharmant** you need, for a kilo of beef, a quarter of a bottle of Pécharmant and a generous glass of

brandy, eight carrots, a large onion, a whole calf's foot, *bouquet garni*, parsley, pork fat, stock, and salt and pepper. Blanche the calf's foot. Lard the beef and brown it in a casserole. Set fire to the brandy and pour it over the beef. Add the sliced carrots and onion. Quarter the blanched calf's foot and add it to the casserole, along with parsley, salt and pepper, and the *bouquet garni*. Then add the Pécharmant, cooking now quickly (and not leaving the cooker for one instant). Next add the stock – just enough to cover the beef. Boil, and then cover, transferring the dish to a moderate oven. Leave it to cook for about two hours. For the next forty-five minutes baste frequently, finally taking off the lid and watching until the beef is perfectly cooked.

Finally, of course, it should be mentioned that Pécharmant is equal to a strong cheese, like Roquefort or, for that matter, Stilton.

The other great wine of the region, Monbazillac, is one of the sweetest white wines in the world. It is produced south of the river, due south of Bergerac, in a vineyard of 2,530 hectares washed by a stream known as La Gardonette. The varieties of grape are the same as for Montravel, but the wine they produce here is unique. This is hot country in summer. The chalky-clay soil makes the grapes luscious. The morning mist moistens the growing grapes and then disappears to let the sun swell them. All this continues till very late in the autumn when the fungus *Botrytis cinerea* – called by the locals the 'noble rot' – begins to attack the grapes. The skins split, the grapes slowly lose all their water and they shrivel up. Then, very carefully, they are harvested by men and women using special scissors. Often the harvest requires successive pickings. The result is a honey-coloured, unctuous, astonishingly luscious wine, always containing at least 12° of alcohol but sometimes far more, which should be drunk very cold, at around 5°. The best vintages should certainly not be drunk before they are at least five years old and they can be kept without anxiety for up to fifteen years, slowly gathering an amber hue. These are wines that as yet have not been fully appreciated by some connoisseurs. Alexis Lichine judged that 'Monbazillac never attains the quality or complexities of the better Barsac and Sauternes'. Though unfair, such judgments happily help to keep down the price.

If you are going to drink Monbazillac with a meal, the food needs to be matched in strength. It is powerful enough, for instance, to match a cheese as strong as Roquefort. In Monbazillac they recommend drinking their sweet wine with *foie gras*, white meat and poultry. If you drink it with fish, they tell you that the fish is best prepared with a sauce that has a strong base.

One such dish is **Turbot crème gratin**. Boil potatoes that have been cut into slices. Take an oval dish, oil it and place the potatoes, lying one on top of the other, on the base and round the sides to a thickness of two or three centimetres. Cover them with *sauce béchamel*. Cook the fish, cut into chops, drain well and place in two tiers in the middle of the dish. Cover with more *sauce béchamel*. Grate cheese over the top and lightly brush the whole with oil. Cook in a medium oven until the whole dish is golden and the cheese has melted over the surface.

In other regions of France this dish is usually cooked with *pommes duchesse*, not the homely sliced potato. But the plain slices in this version seem to me the perfect complement to the rich sauce.

Monbazillac is also used in fish dishes. Most notably, it beautifully flavours a sea trout. The trout is skinned, cleaned and seasoned, and then placed in a greased fireproof dish, the Monbazillac is added and then the dish is cooked in the oven. This would be served simply with poached, thickly sliced cucumber and the reduced cooking liquor from the fish. However, in a restaurant today, contrary to Dordogne tradition, a few pieces of butter would often be added to thicken the sauce, which is then poured over the fish.

Monbazillac is also used rather unexpectedly in combination with plum *eau-de-vie* and garlic in my favourite recipe for a leg of mutton.

Gigot à la couronne d'ail takes six hours to cook but no more than fifteen minutes to prepare. For six people you need a leg of mutton weighing two kilos, 50 grammes of goose or duck fat, 50 cloves of garlic, a glass of plum *eau-de-vie* (*mirabelle*), two glasses of Monbazillac, salt and pepper. Heat the fat in a deep pan. Put into this pan the *gigot*, turning it from time to time. Put the garlic cloves – in their skins for a very mild flavour or skinned for a stronger taste – in the pan all round the mutton. Pour the *eau-de-vie* over the lamb and light it. Then add the Monbazillac. Salt and pepper. Cover the pan, completely sealing it. In a very slow oven let it cook for five and a half hours. Serve the *gigot* in slices, along with the golden garlic. This dish is often these days accompanied with a purée of broad beans.

Another splendid Périgord use for this *liquoreux* wine is to pour a glass on half a ripe melon, adding a hint of Angostura bitters and some slices of walnut. I once picked up a leaflet at the Maison du Vin, Bergerac, suggesting that Monbazillac also blends splendidly with Armagnac, and since we had a full bottle of Armagnac at home at the time I did not need much persuading to give it a try. It was an interesting combination. But most of all I like to drink a glass of Monbazillac at the end of the day, by itself, as I wind down in front of the fire.

Sometimes, on cold evenings during the long winter months, I indulge instead in the last and quite astonishing speciality of the *département* of sturdy drinkers: an *eau-de-vie*. In Périgord it is still made with the help of an *alembic*, a travelling still visiting the local farmers to transform their grapes, and sometimes apples, into extraordinarily powerful spirit. This is so intoxicating that today the amount any one person may distill for his own use is, supposedly, strictly limited.

Always give visitors small glasses. Last Christmas one of my Dordogne neighbours brought as a present a bottle of *eau-de-vie*, distilled by himself from prunes. He told me that this particular *eau-de-vie* was twenty years old, and certainly it was bottled in a remarkably ancient lemonade flask. A few days later a couple of English friends came to see in the New Year with us. I took out the bottle of *eau-de-vie* and generously handed it over. Unwisely and unwittingly they each poured themselves an enormous, quietly powerful slug. Inevitably neither guest could finish his glass. Then one of them stood up and – before I could stop him – poured the precious contents of his glass over the almost totally spent logs of my open fire. Huge blue flames sprang up the chimney, as if a pint of methylated spirits had been emptied over the dying embers.

A refinement (or possibly one should say enrichment) of *eau-de-vie* is to add to it berries and soft fruits – bilberries, greengage plums, strawberries, raspberries, juniper berries and cherries. In this region they also, of course, add walnuts. The proportions of straightforward *eau-de-vie* to combine with the fruit varies with each person's taste.

A large home-produced bottle of **Liqueur de genièvre** (juniper berries), for instance, might well have been created from 60 grammes of fresh berries, a litre of *eau-de-vie* (with an alcohol content of 50°), 200 grammes of crystallised sugar, and a piece of cinnamon. The juniper berries will have been marinated in the *eau-de-vie* for at least two months.

Much secret lore is said to encompass the making of these liquors and their preservation. Certainly, there are endless subtle variations of method. Sometimes, particularly when made with walnuts, red wine or *sirop* is added later instead of sugar with the fruit.

My neighbours make **Liqueur de noix**. They cut green walnuts into pieces, place them in a glass jar, cover them with *eau-de-vie* and leave them to marinate for a couple of months. Then they draw off the alcohol and add to it a clove and cinnamon. A *sirop* made of sugar and water is next prepared, cooked for eight minutes, allowed to cool, and then added to the walnut liqueur. Red or *rosé* wine may also be added. The mixture is stoppered, and allowed to macerate for a further three or four months. Finally the liquid is strained and put into bottles.

Also known as *brou-de-noix*, this is not a drink to be trifled with or over indulged in. But it does loosen tongues and make for merriment. When our neighbours merrily add some to the cups of black coffee we are drinking, I frequently wonder whether I shall make it back up the slight slope that leads to our house. If you wish to try making these liqueurs, vodka is probably the best substitute for *eau-de-vie*.

The habit of spicing peasant food with *eau-de-vie* still pleasingly persists in Périgord. Twenty-five years ago a lover of this region, Philip Oyler, described how chestnuts were cooked and mashed in a peasants' household. He added: 'Our local *auberges* (whose cooks are such artists) generally serve it mashed with some *eau-de-vie* and sprinkled with a little ripe sugar.' You are still offered mashed chestnuts, flavoured exactly like this, in the countryside of our part of Périgord.

Traditionally, too, it is used in fruit preserves. One recipe dissolves twenty lumps of sugar in a bottle of Monbazillac and spices this with a glass of *eau-de-vie*. Plums are bottled in this liquor and left for a month before eating. Less potently, it is often sprinkled over fresh fruit and added to *purées*, *compôtes* and *crèmes*.

⚜

> For a **Crème aux abricots**, you need 300 grammes of ripe apricots, 100 grammes of *fromage blanc maigre* or, if that is not available, cottage cheese, a soupspoon of kirsch, a soupspoon of castor sugar and another apricot for decoration. Peel the apricots, except the one for decoration, and put them in a casserole. Just cover them with water and cook them gently for fifteen minutes (Do not cover.) Put the apricots in a liquidizer to obtain a purée. Add the kirsch and mix. Add the *fromage blanc* to the purée mixture and blend well together. Put into a serving dish and keep in the refrigerator until ready to serve. Decorate with a sliced apricot.

These *eau-de-vie* spiced desserts are offered with a certain merriment and twinkle. Perhaps it is unfair not to add that I first spotted the meaning of the extraordinary gesture, as it were twisting off the end of one's nose, when I was offered mashed chestnuts in *eau-de-vie*.

Invasion and Retreat

'Jesus wept; Voltaire smiled. Of that divine tear
and of that human smile is composed the sweetness
of our present civilization.'

VICTOR HUGO

As one of the most exquisite regions in Europe, the Périgord is
enormously seductive to the tourist. In the main, local people
welcome tourism. It is, after all, the chief industry of a region that
has for decades been coping with major economic and social crises.
Attempts to industrialise parts of the Dordogne in order to retain its
falling population seem scarcely ever to have succeeded: the
workshops set up at Périgueux in 1864 to repair the rolling-stock of
the French railways are one of the few ventures which still employ
people today. Meanwhile other industries have actually declined,
particularly metal works, which in one way or another flourished in
Périgord from Roman times until the mid-nineteenth century. And
today, in spite of immense efforts on the part of the authorities, the
département is still under-industrialised, its factories unable to offer
work to all the young who demand it; the number of industrial
workers only slightly exeeds those still farming. There is some
hydro-electricity; paper-making; lime and cement works near Saint-
Astier; the footwear industry; a gunpowder factory at Bergerac; a
large cheese factory on the outskirts of Périgueux; a timber factory
near Boulazac; and tanneries at Petit-Bersac, Montignac, Saint-
Pardoux-la-Rivière and Sarlat.

It would be foolish to underestimate the problems caused by all this. Against such a background the social impact of tourism is far from bad. First and foremost, the tourists who flood here bring in much needed revenue – to be precise, well over 250 million francs each year.

Alongside that, to discover that strangers appreciate your own cultural and culinary heritage is exhilarating. Tourism has not only encouraged the will, but in many cases has also provided the money to care for that heritage. Take the village of Saint-Amand-de-Coly, whose population fell by two-thirds in less than a century. It is a quite outstanding village in a region of remarkable ones. Saint-Amand-de-Coly in the middle ages was the home of 200 Augustinian monks, who brought employment and wealth to the farmers of the neighbourhood. There, in the twelfth century, they built a massive church. Although only the ramparts of the monastery remain, the church itself is still intact. It survived the Hundred Years' War and the Wars of Religion. The Protestants captured it in 1575, but the monks returned and lived there peacefully till the 1789 Revolution. Their church offered physical as well as spiritual protection. Saint-Amand-de-Coly has an enormous bell-tower, built deliberately like a keep. Only a few holes, out of reach of any attackers, serve as windows. Each façade is fortified. Inside is a massive tower. Here, in case an attacker gained entry, beams enabled the defendants to escape to the tower and shut themselves in. High up on the walls, extending as far as the great dome, runs a footpath from which arrows could be rained down on an unwelcome intruder. This house of God is filled with hidden stairways and hollowed out pillars, ready hiding-places for the beleaguered.

Yet until 1984 Saint-Amand-de-Coly was hard to find, so well hidden between Sarlat and Montignac that even the few tourists who knew of its existence were unlikely to turn aside and find it. This preserved it as a secret pleasure for a few, but it was not so good for the village. Then splendid notices, depicting the massive church, appeared on the D704, persuading the motorist to make a rewarding detour. These had been set up by the villagers themselves. When I praised the proprietor of the village café for their initiative, he asked me had I noticed the box in church asking for gifts towards its renovation (he courteously did not ask had I contributed.) He knows that in his lifetime, at any rate, the village will never repopulate itself. But he told me of the determination of the whole village to bring so many visitors to Saint-Amand-de-Coly that it will be restored – and that soon.

Saint-Amand-de-Coly is only one of many such villages. This is happening throughout the Dordogne. Our village, for instance, has been partly brought to life by outsiders: Parisians, a Dutch family, a distinguished executive of the scent trade, all have secondary residences here, as my family does. The shutters are still closed for far too long in a year. But the place is no longer a sad ruin. In winter the cafés of Domme and its small book and trinket shop are closed. Only one of its three wine shops stays open. In summer the crowds come, and business flourishes.

There are countless other more spectacular examples. Carsac church was in ruin till the 1940s, when it was superbly restored and filled with artistic treasures. The restoration of château Beynac is another instance. This magnificent, medieval fortress sits high up on a limestone cliff, dominating its village below, which can hardly find room for itself between the cliff and the roadway, flanked here by the sharply winding River Dordogne. When Richard Coeur de Lion took the château in 1189, the fortress had been several times rebuilt. Today's buildings rest on the foundations of ruins left twenty-five years later by Simon de Montfort. The keep and the huge Hall of State date from the thirteenth century. In the next century was constructed a tower overlooking the rock itself. The fifteenth century had added to the superb buildings a chapel with frescoes depicting the Last Supper and the Beynac family. The seventeenth century added an Italianate staircase constructed in the Florentine manner.

Happily these survive intact. I look at photographs of the fairly disreputable state to which château Beynac had been reduced before restoration began and marvel at its present beauty. Restoration began, largely under the impetus of tourism, and today you can drive up the twisting road through the village, visit the brutal, magnificent fortress, and look over the rich valley towards châteaux Castelnaud and Fayrac.

One of the great specialities of the region is *lièvre à la royale*, given its regal epithet in the late nineteenth century to honour it as an extraordinary *chef d'oeuvre*. It also has its local variations – now coming to be appreciated by the tourist – one of which is *lièvre à la royale de Beynac et Sarlat*. Overall, I feel this tastes better as well as being quicker to prepare. The hare is cooked in this recipe wrapped in bacon instead of larded with it, which is the more usual technique. The sauce is less heavy too: white wine is used rather than red wine, and neither blood nor bread are added to the sauce.

❦

Lièvre à la royale de Beynac et Sarlat is cooked with a young hare, no more than one year old, a *foie gras* weighing about 750 grammes, truffles, and dry white Bergerac wine. The hare is boned very carefully; the liver is kept apart and made into a forcemeat with other scraps of meat and a glass of Armagnac, the juice of truffles, salt and pepper. The hare is seasoned, wrapped around the forcemeat, and itself wrapped with bacon into which has been inserted thin slices of truffle. On top are placed two slices of the *foie gras*. The hare is cooked slowly in a moderate oven, tied with string. It is served with a reduced sauce made from the bones, the dry white wine, goose fat, garlic, three shallots, a sliced carrot and a sliced onion, a litre of *bouillon* and *bouquet garni*, simmered slowly for at least three hours.

What enormously enhances the pleasure of this gastronomic masterpiece is to eat it under the massive protection of château Beynac.

The achievement in restoring château Beynac can be set against the melancholy, though heroic, attempt of the American-born cabaret star Joséphine Baker to do the same for château des Milandes close by, some forty years ago. Count Harry Kessler, who saw Joséphine Baker dance at a dinner party in Berlin in 1926, 'naked apart from a pink muslin apron', perceptively summed up her allure as 'bewitching . . . but almost quite unerotic'.

'Miss Baker was dancing a solo with brilliant artistic mimicry and purity of style, like an ancient Egyptian or other archaic figure performing in an intricate series of movements without ever losing the basic pattern. This is how their dancers must have danced for Solomon and Tutankhamen.

Apparently she does this for hours on end, without tiring and continually inventing new figures like a child, a happy child at play. She never even gets hot, her skin remains fresh, cool, dry.'

The highest-paid entertainer in Europe, the Charleston queen of Paris, Joséphine fell in love with the Renaissance château during a visit to the Dordogne in the 1930s. During World War II she made it a refuge for resistance fighters and escapees from the Nazis. She fell in love with the food as well as the châteaux of the Dordogne. At Les Milandes she and her husband Jo Bouillon (*sic*) set up a restaurant with a typical patois name, Lou Tornole, meaning 'Please come again'. Here, too, as one who had suffered much racial discrimination as a young girl in St Louis, Missouri, she determined to make Les Milandes a place of harmony among nations, adopting her tribe of 'rainbow children' from all corners of the world. She even obtained the blessing of the Pope for her rainbow tribe and in the newly named Place Joséphine at Les Milandes she set up a statue of the Virgin Mary with a face uncannily resembling her own.

Built by the lord of Castelnaud for his bride, the lovely medieval château was spared during the Wars of Religion, even though its owners were Protestant, and much more had been added in the nineteenth century. When Joséphine Baker bought it, she began to restore its superb terraces and its sumptuous interior. But the money ran out. By the time the debts accumulated by her ambitious project had topped 80 million old francs, château des Milandes had to be desparingly sold. Joséphine Baker is only one of the many British and Americans who fell in love with the Dordogne – to her name must be added those of Rudyard Kipling, the novelist Henry Miller, that superb travel-writer Freda White, the tragic Nancy Cunard, and, as the decades have passed, countless others. The French passion for statistics enabled them to announce that in 1980 tourists spent a colossal total of 3,600,000 nights in the *département*, each person staying here an average of five or six days. I sometimes think that today this region attracts more British and Americans than any other in France. Of course this does have disadvantages. In summer the British seem to have occupied Sarlat again as if the Treaty of Brétigny which gave us Aquitaine had never been superseded. One August I sat outside the Café du Théâtre drinking coffee with my literary agent. 'There', he said, pointing to a man in shorts hand-in-hand with a lady, 'are our countrymen and women at their best.' The pair looked happy. I have never seen a French couple walking hand-in-hand down the Rue de la République, Sarlat's high street. 'That', I replied, 'is no ordinary British couple. That is the Bishop of Blackburn and his wife.' They are old friends and we spent a very pleasant evening together.

Occasionally I get a sneaking suspicion that the whole region has become a subtly disguised playground or *colonie de vacances*. One summer day I was irritated that three coaches were trying (and failing) to get through the Porte del Bos, at Domme, holding me up. Eventually they parked outside and out clambered Italian musicians from the Orchestra of Turin. That evening they were to give a concert in one of Domme's two churches. As a prelude half a dozen of them sat down in the little square high on the 'Bluff' above the River Dordogne, and began to play waltzes. And soon everyone was waltzing in the open air.

There are, of course, far more serious drawbacks. I have often heard people ask for 'civilised' tourism. Virtually every tourist attraction is exploited, sometimes in an unprepossessing way, even by families who still live close to the land: it comes as a surprise, for example, to find in France even prehistoric caves privately owned and exploited. Facilities demanded by the tourists disrupt the local patterns of life. Once – only once – I consented to visit one of the local *boîtes*, discotheques, with my younger daughter and a couple of her friends. For some unfathomable reason the proprieters had thought it a good idea to give a tropical flavour to this discotheque by importing a number of parrots, whose noises tended to drown the music. To get in cost fifty francs – though the price of admission included one free drink. Thereafter further drinks cost fifty francs each (as compared with, say, seven francs in a Sarlat café).

Unfortunately, too, tourists seem so often to underestimate country people. To underestimate the intelligence or the resilience of the French peasant farmer is deeply discourteous. One day I was sitting on my wall when a car with German number-plates came up the narrow road and found itself in a cul-de-sac. The driver and his companions anxiously discussed in German whether they should ask me how they had gone wrong and how to reach the beach. Eventually they addressed me in halting French. It seemed to me better to tell them the way in their own language. The driver of the car who assumed I was French, then astonished me by asking: 'Tell me, how does a French peasant speak such excellent German?' I could perhaps have explained that my neighbour, M. Véril, had learned a little German in Buchenwald.

There are also serious and justified worries that tourism is a precarious prop. The people of the Dordogne know an economy depending on tourism is a strange and partly distorted economy. It is seasonal, at times putting great strain on those who work in a tourist haven, at other times leaving them with little to do. It is not totally under the control of those whose livelihood depends on it. Fluctuations in the weather, in the exchange rate, in holiday fashions can, and do, all effect the prosperity of the region.

Yet on the whole tourism is smiled upon as it haphazardly gathers pace. By 1970 the Dordogne had developed over seventy camp sites with enough room for 11,000 people, as well as 250 rural *gîtes* housing over 1,500 visitors, and more than 500 hotels capable of catering for nearly 10,000 persons at once. A decade later the number of camp sites had doubled, the number of *gîtes* had risen to nearly 850 and the hotels were offering another thousand beds. I am a great advocate of the *gîtes* and other forms of self-catering holiday, but not simply because they are cheaper than staying in hotels. They also give the tourist freedom to be absolutely at ease, without worrying whether other guests are annoyed by one's noisy children or own drinking habits. However, it is foolish not to eat the local food at least a couple of times. It is as much a part of a region's culture as its history, artistic heritage and landscape – and, as a living tradition, one of the few ways of sharing, understanding and showing appreciation of that culture. It is also highly pleasurable. Paul Valéry wrote a poem about regret, using as his image some superb wine (*le vin perdu*), stupidly thrown into the sea. To visit the Dordogne and cook for yourself all the time is to jettison not only fine wine but also *la nourriture périgourdine*.

In virtually every place of note throughout the Dordogne, there is now a *syndicat d'initiative*, or information office. Sometimes these are run professionally. Sometimes they are staffed by charming volunteers. Once I decided to go to look at the fourteenth-century frescoes in the Romanesque church at Coulaures. I got lost and called for information at the Syndicat d'Initiative of Excideuil. Two splendid senior citizens who were looking after it that day gave me a cup of coffee and directions to Coulaures, and reminded me not to miss some of the splendours of Exideuil itself. I came away with a duplicated account of that medieval town, plus a list of local events, concerts, exhibitions and firework displays for the coming summer. The Office Départemental du Tourisme in the Avenue de l'Aquitaine, Périgueux, co-ordinates all this. In the same building is a centre offering endless advice and information to young people touring in the area.

Périgueux, I believe, relishes tourism. Certainly its architectural inheritance is being beautifully restored with the wealth that tourism brings. Few ugly buildings have replaced the heritage of the past. Although certain fine buildings of the past have regrettably been lost, some in this century, the narrow twisting streets of old Périgueux are a legacy of a city that went to sleep for several centuries after the turbulent Wars of Religion. This is still the city of Montaigne, whose statue stands close by that of Archbishop Fénelon in the Allées Tourny, who once observed, 'I should far rather find myself second or third in any venture in Périgueux than first at any in Paris.'

Every street in old Périgueux is redolent with history. Humdrum houses and Renaissance mansions alike have their memories. In the Rue des Farges, for instance, is the house where the mighty Du Guesclin lived when he was re-arming to drive the English out of Aquitaine during the Hundred Years' War. Among the old houses of the Place Daumesnil, close by the cathedral, you find the one where Yrieux Daumesnil, the great general, was born in 1776. Daumesnil lost a leg at the battle of Wagram, and you can see his statue – wooden leg and all – here in the Cours Michel Montaigne. Périgueux thus preserves a dual history: a tradition of peace and a tradition of war. Indeed, Freda White saw this as the essence of its character, describing it as 'an ancient city that shows fewer signs of age than many French provincial capitals.' This she attributed to its singularly troubled history. 'Time and again it was destroyed, only to rise again, because the fertile Isle valley needed á market and centre.'

Périgueux was also once exceedingly poor. In the eighteenth century the poor thronged the old city, begged for bread, pathetically filling the streets between the cathedral and the river.

Country girls came to the city to find a miserable employment as servants, abused by their masters, living in crowded attics, in cellars, even in cupboards. In the late eighteenth century 85% of unmarried mothers in Périgueux were serving-girls.

The most attractive building in the whole city, in my own view, is the ancient mill that fronts the river, which once belonged to the long-disappeared monks and cannons of the cathedral. Now it is a quaint overhanging building that seems to have nothing to do but treasure its memories. Across the river, reflected in the waters of the River Isle, the cathedral gives to Périgueux a curiously oriental, even Byzantine aspect. Today its five magnificent domes and twelve pepperpot towers are breathtaking. Inside is an extraordinary feeling of peace. Light and shade are magically deployed. Great chandeliers, designed by the restorer Paul Abadie, help to give an impression of soaring power.

Whenever I visit Périgueux I like to go backwards in time, so to speak, in the church of Saint-Étienne, by way of the middle ages to the times of the Romans and the Gauls. The present church dates from the eleventh and twelfth centuries. It once had four domes. Today it possesses only two, for the Huguenots who invaded the city in 1575 smashed down the other two. The western dome is the older one of the two that survived. It is also the larger one – some 15 metres in diameter – whereas the eastern dome, finished in 1150 or thereabouts, is only 13.70 metres in diameter. For a long time this church was the city's cathedral. Inside is the finely chiselled tomb of Bishop Jean d'Asside, sculpted in 1169 by mason Constantin de Jarnac. Jean d'Asside rests oddly in a church dedicated to one who committed himself in death to forgiveness since the prelate was a warrior-bishop, ready at any time to take up arms against 'heretics' that he could not convert by reason alone.

Going back in time, St Front himself built the first shrine here, choosing his spot deliberately on the old Roman temple which was dedicated to the God of War. Étienne (Stephen), who died forgiving his enemies, represented the Prince of Peace. Happily, St Front did not obliterate the whole of the Gallo-Roman complex of buildings dedicated to the god of war. Close by the church is the old gateway of the god Mars.

If you walk the other way, north-west of the church, you reach the most charming amphitheatre in France, an arena comparable in size to those at Arles and Nîmes, standing elliptically on axes 153 and 125 metres long. This, too is a journey in time. In the days when the Gauls and Romans exulted over blood and circuses here, the arena was adorned with marble statues of Hercules, Jupiter and Diana on horseback. You walk through tunnels once used by gladiators who were about to fight for their lives. Centuries later, the counts of Périgord built an imposing château on the foundations of this amphitheatre. So hated were these *grands seigneurs* that a revolt of 1391 threw them out of their château, which the populace then rased to the ground. The ruins of the château and amphitheatre were then used as a public quarry, providing rubble and stone for buildings elsewhere. By the mid-nineteenth century the arena was in a sorry state, trees and creepers threatening what still remained. Today it is in splendid order, restored as a children's playground, frequented by mothers with prams and young boys and girls paddling in a shallow, pretty pool.

Next to the arena are the well-preserved Gallo-Roman walls of the old city, built towards the end of the third century in an attempt to defend the city against the barbarians, with the so-called 'Norman' gateway and the château Barrière, now an impressive ruin. The 'Norman' gateway is in fact the one surviving Roman gateway to the ancient city of Périgueux, while the château Barrière was the home of an extraordinary militant noblewoman, Jeanne de la Barrière, who achieved fame in 1369 by rallying the defenders of her other château, de Reilhac near Le Bugue, against the attacks of the English. Constructed in the twelfth century on one of the ancient towers of the old Roman wall, the château Barrière was burned down by the engraged Huguenots in 1575.

Walk south from the château Barrière and you reach the remains of an extraordinary pagan temple, the tower dedicated to Vesunna, the goddess under whose protection the city once lived. This tower, 20 metres in diameter and 27 metres high, was once covered in marble. It remains impressive today, even though one side is partly smashed down. The Christians were quick to use this damage to argue the superiority of their faith: the legend grew that St Front threw a demon out of the tower of Vesunna so powerfully that the evil creature ran through the wall in his attempt to escape the vengeful Christian.

Just by the astounding cathedral, you can buy vegetables and other food every Wednesday and Saturday at the main market held in the Place du Clautre; another, smaller market is set up every morning in the Place du Cloderc. Buying Dordogne vegetables in the shade of a cathedral is entrancing to my mind. Eating out of doors is also a great treat in summer in Périgueux. The Place Saint-Louis in Périgueux possesses a fountain in the shape of a fat lady (who looks to me more like a toad) and an *hôtel* with a round tower-stairway and curiously battlemented walls, whose doorway has a twisting Renaissance shell. Here you can sit at tables and make merry in the sun after wandering round the market. I like to watch *la circulation* and sip a sorbet – lemon or orange or even passion fruit.

The restaurateurs of Périgueux are particularly fond of cooking with Dordogne wines. The chef at the Chez Léon in the Cours Tourny, for instance, is proud of his *filet de truite saumonée* in Monbazillac. One speciality often served here among the *plats régionaux* is *le poulet rouilleuse*, so named from the *sauce rouilleuse* in which the chicken is served. The adjective *rouilleuse* (rusty) refers to the chicken blood from which the sauce is made. Curnonsky declared, 'This rust-coloured *sauce rouilleuse*, which goes so well with hare and rabbit is the pride of Périgord.' For many years I refused to try it. Now that I have done so I agree with him.

♣

His own recipe for chicken with **Sauce rouilleuse** simply tells you to keep the chickens' blood when you kill them. For this you need a home-killed chicken or consultation with the butcher. For one chicken you also need two tablespoonfuls of goose fat, 450 grammes of small, white onions, which you keep whole, 1½ tablespoonfuls of flour, half a cup of chicken stock, slices of toast, a clove of garlic, salt and pepper and – not least – half a cup of chicken blood. Cut the chicken into pieces and sauté them in the fat. Cook for another fifteen minutes until they are brown. Add the onions and the flour and a little lukewarm chicken stock. When the chicken is cooked, mix the half cupful of blood with the cooking liquid and heat it without bringing to the boil. (If it does boil it will curdle). Serve the flesh of the chicken on the toast, which you have lightly rubbed with garlic. Garnish with the small onions.

To travel even further back in time, head for the valley of the River Vézère, where prehistoric caves and shelters abound. In them life long ago is perfectly evoked by surviving cave drawings, sometimes coloured, sometimes in brown ochre; by etched animals – many, such as Siberian leopards or woolly mammoths, totally disappeared from this region and even from the face of the earth; by the tools and the still blackened fireplaces hewn by these prehistoric people. Here is the evidence that long ago bears, bison and the now extinct wild ox roamed these valleys. The cavern of Rouffignac, for instance, contains drawings of twenty mammoths, nine bison, seven horses, three rhinos, and eleven ibex in the principle chamber alone. In another part of the cave two herds of mammoths, seven against four, battle in unequal combat. Here our earliest ancestors made their home.

Almost uniquely, the general public is still allowed to visit many of these caves and ancient shelters. To do so is to uncover layers of history that have come between ourselves and these ancestors of mankind. The greatest of these, Lascaux at Montignac, was closed to all save scholars over twenty years ago. In compensation for this, the French in 1984 opened a remarkable replica of part of the Lascaux caves at Montignac, close by the original. The capital of French prehistory is the town of Les Éyzies-de-Tayac. Here, in 1868, were discovered the bodies of 'Cro-Magnon' man, along with his wife and child. Their bones had been undisturbed for 35,000 years; today 300,000 tourists visit Les Éyzies annually. Nearby is the cavern of le Grand Roc, with its marvellous crystalline structures, stalagmites and stalactites. There are also the amazingly well-preserved prehistoric shelters at Carpe Diem, La Madeleine, Laugerie-Basse or Laugerie-Haute, and I would recommend, near Le Bugue, the underground cave of Bara-Bahau, with its extraordinary drawings, and another cave, the Gouffre de Promeyssac, with odd concretions and translucent stalagmites and stalactites.

The other great town of the Dordogne, Sarlat, transports the visitor to medieval rather than Roman times. It, too, has blossomed with tourism. In 1853 a French observer declared that 'The old town has a sad, desolate aspect; the streets are narrow, the houses black and covered in stone.' For two hundred years, from the late seventeenth century, it more or less slept. Revolts and revolutions seem almost to have passed it by. Even when it lost its bishop, he became mayor instead. The most important public events of the nineteenth century seem to have been the cutting of the long straight Rue de la République, known locally as La Traverse, through the rabbit warren of medieval streets in 1837, the building of the abattoir in 1867 and the coming of the railway in 1880.

Today, of course, the city has quite a different effect on the visitor. Henry Miller, visiting the town just before World War II, felt himself passing along the ancient walls of the city 'into the very heart and bowels of the middle ages.' He walked down the narrow twisting lanes, observing here and there a huge medieval or Renaissance doorway. It was, he felt, a gentle place. 'And yet,' he added, 'the background was sombre, massive, almost sinister in its medieval puissance. It reminded me somehow of the *fleur-de-lys* on the heavy escutcheons of the knight errant – that contrast between the heart and the fist, that shook of ancient battle in which the death-blow came as an act of grace and deliverance. It reminded me too of the plagues and the rejoicing which must have followed during the all too brief lulls.'

Sarlat is certainly ancient. Clovis, King of the Franks, granted monks the right to settle here, on the banks of the trickling River Cuze, towards the end of the fifth century. Here were sheltered the relics of St Sacerdos, and of his mother St Mondane. Charlemagne enriched the town. Benedictines built an abbey here in the eleventh century. St Bernard preached here against heretics in 1147. The place was growing in size and importance. Size and importance brought quarrels – the spiritual leaders tussling with the secular for control over the town. During the Hundred Years' War Sarlat remained faithful to the King of France, and was therefore lucky to have been spared by Simon de Montfort in his drive south to crush the Albigensian heretics in the early thirteenth century. When this Hundred Years' War (which lasted much longer) began again in earnest in 1337, Sarlat managed to resist the English until ceded by the Treaty of Brétigny. Two years later the town responded to the appeal of Jean d'Armagnac to turn against the army of the Black Prince. Again and again the forces of England were repulsed.

The heart and the fist coexisted in the town. Pope John XXII had elevated Sarlat to a bishopric in 1317, and forty or so Bishops of

Sarlat reigned spiritually over the diocese till it was dissolved in 1790. But the Sarladais did not escape the horrors of the Wars of Religion. The Huguenot captain Geoffroy de Vivans captured the town on Shrove Tuesday 1574. He held it for no more than three months, but during that time priests were murdered and the relics of St Sacerdos and his saintly mother ground into dust. After the Huguenots had been expelled from Sarlat, a second attempt by Protestants to take the city was mounted in November 1587. Viscount Turenne attacked the walls of the town with a powerful force. Bishop Salignac-Fénelon led the defence of the city. Turenne was repulsed. The occasion was celebrated by a soldier in one of the worst poems I have read. The refrain runs:

> *Turenne, tu n'entreras,*
> *Mais plutôt tu creveras*
> (Turenne, you shall not enter,
> But soon you will die)

The Sarladais apparently loved to chant the many verses of this poem to remember their victory. Surrounding the town are boulevards which follow the route of the ramparts of Sarlat, levelled and filled in a century and a half later. During the seventeenth century the town managed to remain loyal to the kings of France, even though the Frondeurs took the town for three months in 1653. It was in the following century that the city at last felt itself at peace with the world and went into its deep, long sleep.

As at Périgueux, the past is preserved here in the architecture of the town, which is seen best by a lengthy tramp around the twisting streets. Climb to the Présidial, the seat of justice from the sixteenth century to the time of the Revolution; marvel at the early sixteenth-century house of La Boétie, a building half-Italianate, half-Périgourdin; wander by the fourteenth-century Hôtels Plamon and de Maleville; lament the present ruinous and secularised state of the medieval church of St Mary; rejoice at the excellent restoration of the fourteenth-century chapel of the Pénitents Bleus and eye suspiciously the countless bits of saintly bones preserved and put on show in the seventeenth-century chapel of the Pénitents Blancs.

Sarlat cathedral is an oddity, harmonious yet extremely difficult to date. This is because each bishop seems to have taken it into his head either to build a new part or pull down an old part. Sometimes a bishop would do both. In 1706, for instance, a twelfth-century portal at the west end was demolished to make way for the present entrance – the only part of the cathedral that I dislike. A native of Sarlat in 1853 described it as 'characterless, its execution heavy, an architectural anachronism.' This is entirely true.

The destruction of the Romanesque doorway in 1706 is further to be lamented because nearly every other twelfth-century feature of this building was in such a state of disrepair after the Hundred Years' War that the bishops decided to rebuild almost completely. The belltower dates from 1150, but on top of this a quaint, bulbous dome was added in 1740. The rest of the building is powerfully Gothic. The choir was started in 1505 and vaulted in 1682. Three years later the nave and its adjoining chapels were completed. I think it fortunate that Sarlat remained something of an architectural backwater in those days and that masons and architects here were still building in the old Gothic fashion. The interior of the cathedral is very impressive. Massive pillars support an ogive-vaulted roof.

If you go into Sarlat cathedral outside the times of divine service or secular concerts, do not miss the artistic treasures in the little chapels; retables carved in the seventeenth and eighteenth centuries with scenes from the New Testament; eighteenth-century reliquaries in gilded wood; a *pieta* carved in stone in 1648; the wooded pulpit, with its carvings of the four evangelists, and the sculpted stalls of the canons, all dating from the seventeenth century.

Few events in summer give greater pleasure than the concerts in this fine building. In 1770 the organ-builder Jean-Baptiste Cliquot put a splendid instrument into Sarlat cathedral. Recently restored, it brings a succession of famous organists to give recitals. The seasoned church-goer, knowing that hard pews are tolerable only in small doses, takes his own cushion to these concerts.

The delightful Renaissance building that abuts on the cathedral and was once the bishop's palace is also used for concerts. In 1984 I heard there musicians from Toronto. One interesting feature of this particular concert was the programme, with its elaborate comments on each item, especially since the musicians decided to abandon it altogether and play an entirely different set of pieces.

Sarlat food is as rich as the town itself, and it would be wrong not to leave time to eat here. 'The Sarladais,' wrote the American expert Waverley Root, 'a little triangle of land between the Vézère and the Dordogne in the south-east corner of the Périgord, clustered about the town of Sarlat . . . shares with Périgueux, capital of the Périgord, the honor of providing the best food in the territory.' Today the word *sarladais* used as an adjective in menus, still signifies the acme of Dordogne cooking and for many people, including myself this, rather than Périgueux, is the gastronomic capital of the region.

The word *sarladais* on a menu is never a pretentious description. The humblest recipe can be dignified by this adjective. Thus, for example, Jacquou le Croquant's miserable *mique* is the ancestor of today's prized dumplings.

For **Miques sarladaises** mix 250 grammes of bread-crumbs with three eggs, adding salt and pepper. Cut up finely 125 grammes of bacon, adding these to the egg and breadcrumbs mixture. Roll it into balls and roll these in flour. Cook for quarter of an hour in boiling *bouillon*. The *miques* will swell as they cook, and excellently comple-ment meats and vegetables.

You will find in Sarlat an abundance of fine restaurants – one of which, the Auberge de la Lanterne, takes its name from the gloomy tower nearby. The chef is especially proud of the fish courses. There is also the Hôtel Saint-Albert, where I came across *cailles aux raisins*, quail served with grapes. This, however, seems to me far more a dish of the Loire Valley or Provence, where they frequently mingle meats and game with fruit, than the Dordogne.

Sarlat is only one of the extraordinary medieval towns of this region. There are also the twenty-three *bastides* – the towns founded in medieval times with the express purpose of creating peaceful communities which would thrive economically. It was not suffi-cient simply to build a new town in the violent thirteenth century. You had to persuade men and women to go to live there, men and women who would remain loyal supporters of your own authority. So, the new towns offered a remarkable measure of independence and equality to anyone who came there as citizens. None of these new towns was built with a château, for no overlord was to dominate the citizens, and the houses were nearly all exactly the same as the rest. The founders of the town were given the right of self-government, appointed their own consuls and claimed jurisdiction over the parishes and hamlets surrounding the town, whose inhabitants in time of need would themselves find shelter inside the massive walls.

The great Dordogne novelist Eugène Le Roy took one of the bastides, Domme, as a symbol of the egalitarianism that was later to be one of the three banners of the French Revolution. He wrote of it, 'The distinctions of class were scarcely visible in this small town. Thanks both to its isolation and the difficulty of access which repelled strangers, something had survived of the original equality of the inhabitants, created by their early charters and by the way the land had been shared out.' Le Roy also believed that the daily exercise of climbing the steep slopes leading to this *bastide* had given the ladies of Domme the finest legs in Périgord.

Domme remains one of the finest of the bastides, set high on its seemingly impregnable hill called, by the locals, the Acropolis of Périgord. The rock first sheltered Albigensian heretics from their persecutors. They built a château here, and at the other end a *seigneur* of Gourdon built another. Then Philip the Bold ordered his supporters to build a *bastide* here. Three gateways, powerful walls, streets as close to a grid pattern as the lie of the land permitted and the sheer drop from the bluff of Domme to the River Dordogne should all have made the *bastide* the most secure in Aquitaine. Yet the English took the town in 1383; subsequently driven out, they re-took the town ten years later. Not till 1421 did the French succeed in holding on to the *bastide* for good.

If you put some francs into a strange device close to the 'bluff', a recorded voice points out features of the superb panorama and also tells you how Geoffroy de Vivans, the Huguenot leader, captured Domme by daring and trickery in 1558, during the Wars of Religion. Since the recorded voice gets the story wrong and it is a good story, it is worth setting down the true version of the events. Again and again Geoffroy tried and failed to capture the *bastide*. He obtained what he took to be keys to one of the great gates, only to find that he had been tricked: the keys were counterfeit. He tried to climb another gate with ladders in the early morning, but his men failed in the attempt. Finally he decided to attack the *bastide* from the most difficult approach – up the steep bluff itself. Twenty-seven men, led by one Sieur de Péchanaut, scaled the cliff. They hacked the guard to pieces, blew trumpets to put terror into the hearts of the inhabitants, took the keys of the great gate from the Consuls, and let Vivans in. The tale has a curious end. Four years later Vivans decided to change sides in the Wars of Religion, and sold Domme to the Catholics for 40,000 *livres*.

It is also possible to make a round trip around two of the other finest *bastides*: Monpazier and Eymet, which lies in the south-west corner of the *département*. Monpazier stands virtually as it was built, a completely new town founded in the year 1285 by Jean de Grailly, seneschal of Gascony. Deep in the heart of France he was in fact the ally of the Duke of Aquitaine, King Edward I of England, and he designed the new town as a bastion of English authority. Looking in the future in the hope of better times, Jean de Grailly called the town 'the hill of peace', '*le Mont de la Paix*', but this was a turbulent era and he built the town fully expecting trouble.

Monpazier is built as a rectangle, surrounded by walls 220 metres long from east to west and 400 metres long from north to south. Two fortified gates guard the only entrances to the new town. Inside, the town is rigidly designed on a grid-like pattern. Did its builders consciously model their plans on the old Roman defensive towns, with absolutely straight streets, crossing each other at right-angles, so that troops could rush from one end to the other without hindrance to stave off any attack? In case of fire – accidental or the work of enemies – between each rectangular house in Monpazier ran a narrow corridor, a mere 27 centimetres wide but enough to limit the danger. The church at Monpazier is dedicated to St Dominic. It was also designed for the physical protection of the inhabitants, should any invader gain access to the town, and – although the building has been extended and altered over the centuries – you cannot help noticing that it is something of a fortress.

Like Monpazier, Eymet dominates the River Dropt. It continued to develop after the thirteenth century. In the next century a château was built and the keep remains today. In the century after that new houses were built in a delightful wattle and daub fashion. And of course the market still takes place in the old arcaded square. If you visit Monpazier for one of its Thursday fairs, you can also take in the Thursday market at Eymet and sample the local *confits*. This is also *cassoulet* country, a reminder that Périgord is (and has always been) part of that much vaster region, the Languedoc – that our patois is basically that of the Languedoc, and that Languedoc food is one of the roots of our own cuisine. Although *cassoulet* is really found only in the southern parts of Périgord, the much plainer *sobronade* found throughout the region is clearly a close relation.

♨

Cassoulet is a marvellous concoction of pork, lamb, sausages and beans. For eight people cut 300 grammes of pork into cubes, season them and put them into a saucepan with an onion, *bouquet garni*, two cloves of crushed garlic, a kilo of soaked haricot beans and enough stock to cover. Boil, cover, simmer for 1½ hours and then add 450 grammes of pork sausages – small ones if possible. Cook for another twenty minutes. Roast until done 1.1 kilos each of pork sparerib and shoulder of lamb from which the butcher has taken out the bone. Cut into pieces. Drain the beans, keeping the liquid but not the onion and garlic. Into an ovenproof dish put half the beans, cubed pork and sausages. Add the roasted lamb and pork, 5 tablespoonfuls of the liquid and then the beans, pork and sausages that remain. Cover with a 10-mm layer of breadcrumbs. Cook for two hours in an oven at 275°F, adding more liquid to prevent the dish drying up. Serve hot. A Périgord *cassoulet* will also often have added to it some *confits* or sliced *cou d'oie farci*.

If we are too early to eat at Eymet we drive our friends back to Beaumont. Beaumont, it is said, was built in the form of a letter H in honour of King Henry III, Plantagenet ruler of England and Aquitaine. It has all the features of a true *bastide*: a powerful gateway grooved for a long disappeared portcullis; a fortified church with the head of King Edward I amongst the carvings over its west porch; and a market square with its medieval market hall. It is also possible to extend the round trip by driving on to, say, Lalinde, a *bastide* built in 1267 on the orders of King Edward III of England, and Molières, then returning home by way of the superb monastery at Cadouin, west of Molières.

For some reason, many guide books underestimate the charm of Bergerac. One major guide, for example, devotes less than half a page to the town, scarcely pausing over what are virtually dimissed as 'the characteristic lanes of the older town, . . . the vaulted cellars of the Couvent des Recollets . . ., and several other tastefully restored buildings of minor interest.' This is unfair. Bergerac is, after all, the third principal town of the region and a lovely place to visit. I can think of only two good reasons for its unfair treatment: the similar attitude to its wines and the fact that it is just a little way off the beaten track.

A trip to Bergerac is pre-eminently a journey back into the eighteenth century, although its buildings, too, read back to the medieval centuries. Everywhere the charm of the past blends with a bustling modern town that displays but has not despoiled its old inheritance. A shop selling porcelain to tourists is built over an ancient sluice that controls a headlong underground tributary of the Dordogne. Medieval houses, constructed of narrow bricks and beams, overhang the streets. One houses a museum of sacred art. A girls' school occupies what was once a convent church founded in 1260 by Dominican friars from Paris. The convent itself is now the local prefecture. In between 1260 and today this convent was destroyed by the English during the Hundred Years' War; rebuilt, and once more destroyed by local marauders in the second half of the fourteenth century; rebuilt, and then destroyed by the Huguenots in the late sixteenth century; rebuilt again in the early seventeenth century and finally acquired by the civic authorities at the time of the French Revolution.

Many street names in Bergerac evoke the past. There is an unpretentious square named Place des Petites Boucheries. Walk down the Rue Sainte-Catherine and you find, at no. 39, the house where the philosopher Maine de Biran was born in 1766. It is now a doctor's surgery. Maine was a fine philosopher but slightly awry in his personal life. He married his childhood sweetheart and then found that her first husband wanted her back. The affair ended happily for Maine, since she suddenly died of a brainstorm and he married one of her cousins. Maine lies buried in the church cemetery of a village east of Bergerac, Saint-Sauveur, amidst the vineyards of Pécharmant.

The former Couvent des Recollets now houses the wine museum of Bergerac and is home of the Wine Consuls of Bergerac. Here you can see the Wine Consuls' sumptious robes and, on special occasions, witness their amazing ceremonies. Walk up the Rue des Recollets to the square with a modern statue of Cyrano de Bergerac. Cyrano here looks quite noble, in spite of his large nose, drawing his sword among a grove of sweet chestnuts. A notice points you left to the shady cloister and museum.

Follow the Rue de L'Ancien Pont to reach the entertaining national museum of tobacco in the Maison Peyrearede, Bergerac. Here you can learn painlessly the history of tobacco in France. One André Thivet apparently introduced it into Angoulême in 1566. Earlier, Jean Nicot – whose name persists in the word 'nicotine' – supplied powdered tobacco to the Cardinal de Lorraine, who gave it to Catherine de Medici to cure her headaches. This alleged property of tobacco is alluded to in one amusing nineteenth-century lithograph on display here. A suitor, calling on a young lady, notices a cigar stub in her room. 'It seems that someone else has already called on you,' he observes darkly. 'No sir,' protests the girl. 'I smoked it because of my toothache.' Other exhibits are similarly surprising: contemporary pictures depicting redskins smoking pipes of peace and Virginians growing tobacco in the early years of modern America; African statuettes showing black men smoking long pipes; oil paintings of serious gamblers, puffing away; water-colours of ladies demurely smoking; a collection of pipes from as far away as Istanbul; snuff boxes; cigar cases, picturesque tapestries dedicated to glorifying tobacco. Everything is laid out to constitute a paean of praise for the cigar, the cigarette and the pipe.

We take our guests on a trip to Bergerac on Wednesdays or Saturdays, so that they can savour the busy twice-weekly markets. On a warm day in September you can see people selling shiny *cèpes* outside the stern, gloomy Gothic cathedral. Throughout the year you can buy clothing, jewelry, berets, and of course succulent vegetables in the market to the north of this cathedral. Don't be put off by its gloom from going inside the cathedral, if only to hear its organ, which someone always seems to be playing when I am there, and to try to make out the sixteenth-century Italian paintings of the shepherds and Magi adoring the infant Jesus. Directly opposite the west door of the cathedral is the pedestrianised Grand' Rue, which leads to another market, half covered, half open-air. The merchants still often use the old-fashioned hand-held weighing machines of the kind we discovered in our old barn. Live hare and rabbits are also on sale. This is an area known for its *civets*, game *ragoûts* in which the blood of the animal, typically hare or rabbit, is added to the sauce. Since this requires long and messy preparation. I think it is a dish better left to a restaurateur.

Civet de lièvre is prepared here by cutting up the flesh into pieces and marinating them in brandy, oil, salt, pepper and sliced onions. Then diced lean bacon that has been blanched is fried in goose fat with quartered onions and sprinkled with flour. The hare pieces are added, to be sautéed. You must stir the dish continuously, keeping it moist with red wine, adding garlic and herbs, before covering the pan and cooking slowly. A sauce is made from the blood of the hare, its liver – cut into small slices – and mushrooms. The sauce is poured over the hare before serving, and the meat is surrounded with croûtons.

A *civet quercynois*, from the neighbouring departement, will always be flavoured with tarragon.

I would not dare conclude this chapter without admitting how much I have left out. The places and *plats régionaux* I have managed to mention represent but a few of the enchantments of the Dordogne, and in detail I have described only the three principal towns of the Dordogne. Yet this is as much an area of villages and small towns: Saint-Amand-de-Coly, where we began, is only one of many deserving description. Take Excideuil, near the town of Sarrazac, for example. Although it claims to be no more than a village, it is dominated by two massive square keeps, built in the fourteenth century and deriving from a château that belonged to the famous Talleyrand-Périgord family, then to Henri III, and then to a couturier, François de Cars, who spent part of his wife's dowry on transforming the old feudal castle into a lovely Renaissance home. Excideuil also boasts an old Benedictine priory with a splendidly carved doorway, as well as sturdy ramparts.

And the same is true of the small towns: places like Montignac, Nontron and Le Bugue. At Montignac, for example, you can visit the old priory church, a lovely building begun in the twelfth century and embellished for five hundred years. You can visit the remarkable château de la Grande-Filolie, half medieval fortress, half civilised Renaissance home. You can see the house where Eugène Le Roy died on the Rue 14 juillet and visit the museum set up to keep alive his memory in the Rue septembre. And you can enjoy the Wednesday markets.

Then there are the remarkable saints' villages. Saint-Martial-Viveyrol due east of Brantôme on the north-west border of the Dordogne, with its gaunt fortified church; Saint-Pardoux-la-Rivière on the River Dronne south-east of Nontron with its ruined Dominican convent; Saint-Pompont south-west of Domme on the River Lousse, with its medieval châteaux, its ancient houses, its Gothic church with an enormous square belltower; Sainte-Trie north-east of Hautefort, sheltering a ruined Cistercian abbey where once lived the troubadour Bertrand de Born; Sainte-Nathalène, with its imposing Romanesque church, fifteenth-century manor and splendid pigeon-loft; Saint-Félix-de-Bourdeilles; Saint-Astier, where the bones of the sixth-century hermit Asterius rested till 1652, when the Frondeur Balthasar pillaged the place and threw them away; Saint-Vincent-le-Paluel with its Romanesque church where there is a fine wooden reredos, rustically carved, and fifteenth-century manor house. The list could be much longer.

The list of *plats régionaux*, could also be much longer. Capon *truffé*, turkey *truffé* and *ballotine* are just a few of the classic dishes that appear on menus in the most humble of villages as well as in the large towns of the Dordogne. In the end, however, no matter how long the list, the table of Périgord is best described not as a catalogue of recipes, but as an approach to food.

Experts have for a long time distinguished two sorts of cuisine: that of the housewife and that of the chef. As I hope to show, I do not think this distinction is so sharp today as many believe.

À Table!

'A meal is a veritable symphony, truly orchest-
rated, which must harmonise with the total
ambience of the feast.'

PAUL BALARD

Few hotels in the Dordogne are impersonal concerns, run simply as
efficient places for eating and sleeping. Most have family roots. In
very many the proprietor likes to chat and joke, to give advice, to
pass the time of day. If you begin to frequent one with any
regularity you soon become a friend. There is a similar crossover in
the restaurants. In some of the working men's eating places,
customers come into the dining room as if by right, place their
berets on a hook and take their own rolled-up napkins from their
customary place. At others the farmer and his wife cook for their
guests and join them at table.

In the kitchens of both homes and restaurants, too, there is a
characteristic care for quality and detail, and a refreshing lack of
pretentiousness. Frequently hoteliers proudly put the emphasis on
'*des plats simples à des prix sages*' – simple dishes at sensible prices –
or '*des plats rustiques régionaux pour un bon rapport qualité-prix*' – the
right balance of quality and price. In Périgord *noir*, certainly the
fishermen are for the most part planning to take their catches home
for cooking that day. And many local restaurants grow their own
herbs to garnish the dishes of their customers. One very cold
Christmas, for example, we went out to eat in Grolejac. My wife

ordered fish garnished with sorrel. The *patronne* went to the kitchen
and returned full of apologies. The sorrel in the garden had frozen.
Another day I told the chef there how much I had liked his fine
vanilla soufflé. He hastened to tell me that he had not created it
himself and brought to our table a smiling widow named Marie.
She had cooked the soufflé and offered it to the hotel. Two days
later she arrived by car in our village, bringing a vanilla soufflé
made for us. Nor is this exceptional. I know of several restaurateurs
who bake their own bread to accompany their meals.

Everywhere is evident the twin-sided Dordogne tradition of
good food: on the one hand the splendour of the great châteaux and
their cuisine, and on the other careful husbandry of the old peasants,
who had to eke out a precarious existence in spite of the generous
earth that supported them. Even more revealing, Dordogne hotels
also serve with pride dishes eaten only by the very poor in past
years. Take the *mique*, which for Jacquou le Croquant symbolised
the utterly abject life led by his kind, at the best a way of enhancing a
thin soup for the poor, at worst eaten cold by itself. It can be found
today in the country kitchens of the Dordogne and in its many fine
restaurants, still offered as a Dordogne delicacy. Gastronomes
suggest that you prepare it with a mixture of two sorts of corn:
wheat and maize, so as to produce a finer meal. They should be well
mixed with a tablespoon of fat and a glass of warm water, salt and
pepper, then shaped in the palm of the hand into dumplings which
look like oranges. Each *mique*, or several at once, should be boiled in
salted water. When they are cooked (after about half-an-hour) they
should be dried in linen and eaten hot. The old way was to eat them
with cabbage or with either hare or rabbit, but later, specialised
cookery books of Périgord refined the recipe. You can read about
fried *miques*. These are plunged into very hot walnut oil. Some
chefs recommended serving them with vanilla sugar, with honey or
with red currants.

A similar delight – rye bread used to thicken soup – can still be
found in many country restaurants. Just across the river from where
we live is the Restaurant de la Ferme of M. Maurice Escalier. M.
and Mme Escalier not only serve *la soupe au pain de seigle*. They also
proudly advertise the fact in the renowned magazine *Gastronomie
Périgord*. To an Englishman there is a special pleasure in such a soup.
As a child, my parents would never allow me to dip my bread in the

soup, let alone break it into pieces and dunk it. Now I have become a man and put away childish things, the restaurateurs of the Dordogne actually dunk the bread, or *tremper la soupe* as they say locally, for me. And the restaurants of this region are also, in my experience, the fastest in Europe for bringing more bread to dunk or wipe your plate when they spot that you have used it all up.

The greatest gastronomic contrast to my mind exists between the restaurants of a big city and those of a small town. An English spinster, Miss M. Betham-Edwards, who visited the region with a companion in the early years of this century commented that 'The hotels of Périgueux, chief town of the departement of the Dordogne, are not engaging. My travelling companion and myself were enamoured of the old city, its picturesque ways, its sweet limpid river, its Byzantine cathedral, its noble statues of that wonderful pair, Montaigne and Fénelon, its tempting bookstalls and pretty promenades. But we could not, like Falstaff, take our ease at our inn, so we steamed by tramway to Brantôme.' Here, she wrote, 'For two francs per head we fared on trout, partridge – the month was September – and had the offer of too many dishes to remember, our hostess and her daughter seeing to our comfort in every particular.' Indicatively, *Le Chabrol*, the restaurant at Brantôme of which she was writing, still survives. The trout is indeed excellent.

Only a year or two before Miss Betham-Edwards made her trip, Eugène Le Roy described an imaginary Dordogne *bastide*, in his story *La Belle Coutellière*. It is midday. 'On the high rocky plateau, the old royal *bastide* of Montglat-du-Périgord is taking lunch.' No-one is to be seen. Two hours later the people start to come out into the streets again. 'Now the town has awakened,' wrote Le Roy.

In my opinion he underestimated the time you need for a proper Dordogne meal. This is a country of long, long lunches, and it makes more sense to allow an extra half-an-hour. It is is also unwise to arrive for lunch late when you visit a Dordogne restaurant. By half-noon the countryside is quiet where we live, perhaps even earlier. Traffic disappears from the winding roads. Everyone is eating. If you are late, usually you will be found a place. But you disappoint the restaurateur, who wonders why you will not devote the proper time that his cuisine deserves.

At this point comes the most important question of all: what do you drink and eat in a Périgord restaurant? If you do not know your way around a wine menu there there is a trouble-free solution – nearly every hotel and restaurant will have an arrangement with a local *cave-coopérative* to supply its table wine. The restaurant owner himself takes a pride in the fact that this is the wine he recommends to accompany his meals. When the waiter or waitress asks what we want to drink, unless the occasion is extremely special, then I invariably ask for '*la cuvée de la maison*', knowing that it will be an excellent house wine. And if you are ordering one of the meals that working-men regularly eat in those straightforward, down-to-earth Dordogne restaurants where postmen, construction workers, truck drivers, bank managers, old men, widows, policemen and farm labourers sit down on weekdays for their lunch, you will probably find a litre bottle of such red wine already on your table as part of the inclusive deal. Foolishly, I once decided to order a better wine to celebrate my daughter's exam results. The waitress was flung into unusual consternation, but eventually produced a bottle that cost more than everyone's meal added together. We did not greatly enjoy it.

That perceptive lover of Périgord, Freda White, offered excellent balanced advice about wine to the suspicious tourist:

'The traveller need not fear that if he takes the *vin ordinaire* of the menu he will meet that awful bitter red ink for which the hotels of the non-wine-growing provinces charge so dearly. But this does not mean that he should sojourn in the heart of a wine-culture and refrain from tasting the best. He should make a ceremony of drinking some of the great wines; the host of his hotel will advise him as to the best vintage in his cellar, and tell him the right wine to drink with the meal he has ordered.'

One golden rule is to take along a pocket dictionary. When I first began to eat in French hotels I was stupid (or arrogant) enough not to do this. No longer. All French tourist hotels by law must display their menus and prices. With the help of a dictionary you soon perceive that often the cheapest menu is the one most tantalising and appetising. Without a dictionary you might reject *cabillaud* or *morue* out of hand as some possibly dreadful exotic speciality and so miss a delicious cod dish.

Another important guideline – and this applies everywhere in France – is, as far as possible, to eat the dishes of the region and not those of other areas. Sometimes I see Périgord dishes on menus in other regions of France, order them, and wonder why the dish in no way resembles what I eat in Périgord. We once brought some furniture in a van from England to the Dordogne. Feeling uncertain that two of us alone could manage to drive an unfamiliar vehicle all the way, we asked a friend to help. Half way there, in the Loire valley we stopped to eat. He ordered *lièvre à la royale*. When it came I watched him glumly picking at the dish, finally pushing it miserably to one side. The rule should be: in the Loire valley, eat the food of the Loire. In Périgord, eat better.

Beyond these general rules, it is necessary to think of the menu course by course. This approach also seems to me the best way of showing how the twin tradition of the Périgord kitchen translates and reveals itself in food of extraordinary, yet unpretentious quality. First, there will always be soup and always *hors d'oeuvre*. There is no one special Dordogne soup, but there are plenty of good ones. Apart from those already given, sorrel or chestnut soup are both well worth trying. My favourite is broad bean soup.

For **Soupe de fèves** for six people you will need 1½ kilos of broad beans, and a kilo of peas. Traditionally a piece of goose flesh that has been salted and kept for some time adds flavour to this soup. Cook the beans and peas in five litres of water, seasoned, along with the piece of salted goose flesh. Let them cook slowly for about five hours. Serve poured over slices of bread.

You will also often come across a slightly enriched version of a farmhouse *tourain*.

To make the base of **Tourain à la tomate**, heat some oil and in it cook some fresh red tomatoes that you have skinned and chopped, along with some chopped onion. These should cook for fifteen to twenty minutes, and you should salt and pepper them to taste. Next make a *roux* with butter and flour, and mix in water. Add some slices of bread. Pour over the tomatoes and onions.

Next comes the *hors d'oeuvres*, of which a part might be *pâté de foie gras truffé*: this would never, as elsewhere in France and at official banquets, be served at the end of a meal. On a cheaper menu, this could be *rillettes* or a duck *pâté*, which in its own way is just as satisfying a dish as its more expensive cousin. Nor is it considered here as an inferior substitute, rather as a delicious food in its own right.

*

In the Dordogne they make **Pâté de canard** of boned, chopped duck (a 1.5 to 2 kilo bird), 225 grammes of chopped pork fillet, 225 grammes of chicken livers, an egg, garlic, and 225 grammes of belly pork. Mince the belly of pork. Chop the chicken livers. Mix them with the duck, the pork fillet, the egg and the garlic in a bowl. Salt and pepper. Transfer to a medium-sized terrine or ovenproof dish. Cover with greaseproof paper and bake for two hours in an oven at 350°F. Leave to cool, chill and serve with bread.

A *pâté* made entirely from duck or goose liver will be sold as *bloc foie gras*.

There will also be lighter vegetable dishes. Often part of the *hors d'oeuvre* we are served at the Hôtel Plaisance in Vitrac consists of tomatoes, cut like a little basket, the centre hollowed out and stuffed with all manner of delicacies from tuna fish salad to hard-boiled eggs, peas, little diced potatoes and mayonnaise. This, I presumed, must be a fiddly dish found only in restaurants. Not at all. One day Michel Desplat invited me to meet his mother-in-law, whose husband had just died. I walked around and was given a glass of wine. The widow talked to me of her late husband, of his lengthy last days of sickness and of his funeral. All the while, almost unconsciously, she was preparing *les tomates farcies* – feeling them for their quality, cutting them in half, hollowing out the centres, adding some flaked fish and some potatoes, dropping parsley on top. These she put in a frying pan and cooked very gently over a low heat. My taste buds were working overtime and the juices inside my stomach were making me feel weak.

In a restaurant you are more likely to find them served as a cold dish, perhaps as part of *hors d'oeuvres variés*. I find myself so used now to cold *hors d'oeuvres* that the other day in Saint-Omer, in the Pas-de Calais, my taste buds were extremely surprised when the potatoes in oil accompanying my marinated herring turned out to be warm.

🕯️

To make cold **Tomates farcies** for six persons you need eighteen tomatoes weighing 50 grammes each, a flaked smoked trout, 100 grammes of diced ham, 350 grammes of cream cheese, 50 grammes of cubed bread, three tablespoonfuls of olive oil, a teaspoonful of vinegar, two chopped onions, and two tablespoonfuls of chopped parsley. Slice off the tops of the tomatoes and take out the pith in the middle, including all the seeds. Mix the cream cheese in two parts: with the flaked boned trout and with the ham. Season. Bind with mayonnaise. Fry the bread in the olive oil. Mix with the onions, vinegar, salt, pepper and parsley. Fill six tomatoes with the trout mixture, six with the ham mixture, six with the croûtons and onions. Put the tops on again and serve.

You will also find on nearly every menu *crudités*, fresh vegetables which may here include asparagus, green beans and boiled potato.

🕯️

Anyone who supposes that **Crudités** are merely chopped vegetables is utterly mistaken. In this region they are inevitably served with a garlic mayonnaise made from four cloves of garlic, two egg yolks and 300 ml of olive oil, the whole being whisked and seasoned with salt, pepper and vinegar. The vegetables themselves are chopped into *allumettes* (matchsticks) or cubes, and arranged on a plate.

Next on the menu comes the river fish: trout, *friture*, stuffed carp, perhaps grilled pike with a *sauce verte*, eels or perch. The *sauce verte* often served with fish here is made from pounded hard-boiled eggs, mustard, good wine vinegar and oil, with several spoonfuls of chopped fresh herbs and spring onions. You never quite know what way the fish will have been cooked until it arrives on the table; simple dishes without rich sauces are considered the equal of more elaborate presentations. Here are two contrasting ways in which a fillet of sole might arrive.

🔥

For the first, the **Filet de sole** is cut up into little pieces, garnished with salt and pepper and rolled in flour. In a hot frying pan the fish is then sautéed in oil. Artichoke hearts and diced potatoes are then fried together in fresh oil, the fillet of sole is mixed with these and they are warmed together in a frying pan. The dish is served hot, sprinkled with chopped parsley and lemon juice.

The more complex method is to make a *court-bouillon* from the bones of the sole, along with wine, spring onions, rosemary, thyme, parsley, leeks and five crushed tomatoes. This is strained and a little saffron is added. The fillets of sole are folded in two and put in a dish. Some of the *bouillon* is poured over them and they are poached, covered in silver foil. Cream is mixed with the rest of the *bouillon*, which is then reduced until it glazes. The *filets de sole* are served with Hollandaise sauce, along with the glazed *bouillon*, occasionally garnished with slices of lobster.

Another delicious restaurant fish dish, which I first ate at Bergerac, is a *timbale de l'auberge*. In France this is not a difficult dish to make at home since *quenelles* can be bought in the shops.

🔥

For this **Timbale de l'auberge** take some quenelles of pike. Line a savarin mould with them. Poach in steam. To an Hollandaise sauce add some *morels* and cooked tails of crayfish. Empty the mould on to a plate. Pour over the sauce and serve very hot.

If you have chosen a dearer menu you very likely will have the choice of lobster at this point. Cooking lobster is quite hard work and I prefer to let the restaurateurs do it for me; but here is the fashion of the Sarlat region.

♨

For **Homard sarladais** for four people buy two medium-sized lobsters, weighing 1¼ kilos each. You need also oil, two finely chopped shallots, parsley stalks, a sprig of tarragon, a bay leaf, 300 ml of white Bergerac, 40 grammes of goose fat, 25 grammes of flour, 250 ml of milk, two teaspoonfuls of good French mustard, five tablespoonfuls of double cream, salt and pepper and 50 grammes of Gruyère. Split the lobsters in half, lengthways, keeping the shell halves intact. Remove the black intestinal tubes and discard these along with the stomach. Remove the flesh from the shells and the claws and put to one side. Rub the inside of the shells with olive oil. Put the shallots, parsley stalks, tarragon and bay leaf into a pan, along with the wine. Cook until the wine is reduced to about four tablespoonfuls. Melt the fat in a saucepan, stir in the flour and cook for about twenty minutes. Gradually stir in the milk and bring to the boil. Stir this mixture all the time. Add the mustard, wine and cream. Gently heat the sauce. Stir in the lobster flesh, heat gently and season with salt and pepper. Put the lobster back into its shells, and sprinkle on top the grated Gruyère.

Usually there will also be a choice of omelettes for this course. A less expensive menu will offer *omelettes aux cèpes, aux girolles, aux morilles*; a more expensive one *omelette aux truffes*. These should be included in large pieces, not little left-over bits.

Then comes the main course. Here it is varied, always well seasoned, always beautifully cooked. *Plats* in the Dordogne which appear on menus of every price would typically include stuffed chicken, a stew or casserole – *la daube*, a *rouelle* of veal (probably but not necessarily with the treatment specified), a *civet* of hare and finally, the two best known dishes of Périgord, *lièvre à la royale* and *le poulet rouilleuse*. Again, homely food of peasant origin always appears alongside the creations of *grande cuisine*. Let us take three of the country chicken dishes you are likely to find, each of which makes use of very characteristic flavours. A roast chicken often has a deliciously herby mushroom stuffing and the bird is basted with goose fat for additional flavour.

♨

For **Poulet aux champignons** prepare a stuffing of chopped mushrooms, chopped ham and bacon, bread-crumbs, salt, pepper, parsley and shallots that have been finely chopped. Cook quickly in goose fat and bind with an egg. Stuff the chicken to be roasted and cook it with a little goose fat in the pan.

A speciality of the whole of Périgord is *poulet au verjus*, unfermented grape juice. Typically, the same is enriched with the bird's liver and reduced to a glazing consistency.

♨

To cook **Poulet au verjus** you need a fine chicken that has been fed on maize and weighs about 1–1½ kilos. It should be cleaned and plucked and then cut into pieces. Melt in a casserole two soupspoonfuls of goose fat and over a moderate heat sauté six small onions, stirring occasionally. Take them out and discard. In the fat sauté the pieces of chicken, still over a moderate heat. Add two cloves of garlic and a glass of *bouillon*, salt and pepper. Cover and cook gently for fifteen minutes. Take off the heat and add four soupspoonfuls of *verjus* or crab-apple juice. Add two chopped cloves of garlic and the liver of the chicken. Place the casserole over a moderate heat, this time without covering it. The liquid should evaporate until you have left what is essentially a purée. Serve the *poulet au verjus* garnished with grapes.

The third chicken dish you are very likely to be offered in the Dordogne is one that the average British chef or amateur of cooking would probably quail at because of the powerful dose of garlic involved. Such a reaction would be utterly misguided. Garlic that is left in whole cloves, particularly if they are left unskinned and cooked very slowly, has a mild, nutty flavour quite unlike sliced or crushed raw and fried garlic.

♠

To make **Poulet aux gousses d'ail** do not hesitate to match up to twenty cloves of garlic with a chicken weighing 1–1½ kilos. Apart from that, all you need are *bouquet garni*, three tablespoonfuls of goose fat, a bay leaf, half a glass of cognac and salt and pepper. Do not peel the garlic cloves. Use half the fat to cover them in a casserole. Add the chicken, cut into the usual pieces. Season with the bay leaf, salt and pepper and the *bouquet garni*. Cook for forty minutes at 325°F. Take out of the oven, turn the chicken, add more fat and carry on cooking for the same length of time. Flambé with the cognac, strain and serve the chicken hot in a pre-heated dish.

There is also a very good *plat régional, poularde en croûte*, a pie in which the chicken is left jointed in large pieces, as in old English recipes, and mixed with salsify in a fresh tomato sauce. It seems likely that the recipe is one dating from the English presence here.

Game is also certain to be represented on the menu, again in both simple and elaborate ways. 'Simple' when applied to Dordogne cooking, never seems to me quite to mean what it ought to. A pigeon, *en salmis*, is considered a simple dish. It would be cooked thus:

♠

For two **Palombes en salmis** take two pigeons, 100 grammes of ham (not smoked), 50 grammes of goose fat, two onions and two cloves of garlic. Chop the peeled onions and the garlic. Cut each bird into four pieces. Sauté these in the goose fat. Take them out and put in the fat the onions and ham. Add the garlic. Make a sauce separately, using 40 grammes of butter, 40 grammes of flour, four glasses of *bouillon*, one glass of red Bergerac, a *bouquet garni* made from parsley, thyme and a bay leaf, a clove, salt and pepper. Put the pieces of pigeon back into the casserole, along with the onions, ham and garlic. Pour over the sauce and let the dish cook gently for about forty minutes. Place the pigeon pieces on warm serving plates, pour over the sauce, and serve hot.

Cutlets of roe (*côtelettes de chevreuil*), cooked in oil or fat and served with *sauce périgueux*, appear fairly frequently. The tangy sharp flavour needs to be matched by a fairly strong red wine. In other parts of France I have eaten *chevreuil* served in a dish made with juniper berries. So far I have not come across this in Périgord. On the other hand, the restaurateur at the Hôtel du Pont, Grolejac, told me that *chevreuil* is delicious, though fairly expensive, when larded with truffles, sautéed in oil, cooked in a game sauce and Madeira and served with a garnish of artichokes. This dish he dubs *chevreuil Montmorency*. To my mind the one fault of such a recipe is that it does not include half a bottle of dry white Bergerac.

Any Dordogne menu forcibly reminds me how much more these Frenchmen and women appreciate good vegetables than most British people. Apart from *salade verte*, there will always be a small choice of freshly prepared vegetables. The famous Parisian chef Escoffier once wrote that turnip-tops 'are much appreciated in England for lunch'. He was misinformed. We regard turnips as more or less rubbish. It is true that the French word for turnips (*navets*) also means rubbish and is frequently applied to trashy novels and cheap films. But nobody regards the vegetable itself as fit only for cattle. Escoffier himself would blend his turnips with *sauce béchamel*, dubbing this particular dish *navets farcis châtelaine* – turnips stuffed in the fashion of the lady of the manor. In the Dordogne you are more likely to find them succulently served with walnuts.

🔥

The proportions for **Navets et noix** are approximately a kilo of white turnips to 75 grammes of walnuts. Cut the turnips into cubes, blanche them and then simmer in some veal stock. Crush the walnuts and sauté them in walnut oil for five minutes, turning all the time. Then add them to the turnips, seasoning with salt and pepper.

Other good vegetable dishes are sorrel purée and braised endives. They stay white if you simmer them gently in butter and a drop or two of water, covering the dish with greaseproof paper. Often in Périgord you add diced bacon and ham to the endives, along with a little stock.

Next comes the cheese – as always, served before the dessert. Périgord produces a little cheese – around Cubjac, around Thiviers – but alas, this is not a great cheese region and usually you will be offered the cheeses of other regions of France, as well as that made in nearby Roquefort and at Rocamadour. Prince Curnonsky never tired of quoting Cardinal Bourret's remark, 'Roquefort is the King and Pope of cheeses; it is also the cheese of Kings and Popes.' A blue cheese made from ewe's milk, Roquefort, like Monbazillac, depends for its strange perfection on a rare fungus (in the case of the cheese, *Penicillium roqueforti*). There is one local cheese, Échourgnac, from the town of the same name in the la Double forest, but it is not exceptional.

For a dessert, you may well be offered *pâtisserie*, *crêpes*, sometimes waffles, *tartes aux fruits* and *la tourtière*, a delicious local speciality made with layers of paper-thin pastry and prunes flavoured with orange-water. It may also be made with apples, in which case it will be called a *croustade* or *pastis*.

Sorbets and ice-creams have infiltrated everywhere. For a *supplément* we often ask for a *coupe*: an ice-cream garnished with chocolate, syrups, glazed fruits and chantilly cream. Sorbet is a blessing of the age of the freezer. In France it is enhanced by dry white wine – Bergerac of course in the Dordogne.

※

For a **Sorbet** of lemons or oranges, cut the fruit in half, squeeze and strain the juice, and then make up the quantity with wine until you have 250 ml liquid. Sweeten – not too much – and then freeze the mixture, stirring in the edges from time to time. Eventually it begins to resemble a field of slush. Now you must beat it in a food processor or with a whisk. Then freeze again until it is firm.

In summer the fruits of Périgord make the basis of superbly refreshing dishes.

Mousse aux fraises, for instance, requires 300 grammes of strawberries, 100 grammes of castor sugar and the whites of three eggs. Wash and sieve the strawberries, leaving a few for garnishing, and then reduce them to a purée. Beat the egg whites until they are firm. Add the sugar a little at a time, and mix gently. Fold in the egg whites. Put the mousse into a serving dish or individual dishes and decorate with the remaining strawberries.

Strawberries, as we have noted, are replacing some of the declining crops of the Dordogne, so when I am eating them I like to think that I am contributing a little to the economy of the place that so enchants us. They are also delicious in *crêpes*.

To fill a dozen **Crêpes aux fraises,** you need 225 grammes of fresh strawberries, 50 grammes of icing sugar and a little cognac. Toss these together and chill. Divide the mixture to fill each *crêpe*. Fold them, arranging them in a buttered, ovenproof dish. Bake at 200°F for ten minutes. Serve, pouring over the brandy that is left and igniting it.

Finally, I would like to give you the recipe for the delicious vanilla soufflé from the hotel at Grolejac. This is how the widow Marie told us to cook our own.

For a **Soufflé au vanille** for six persons you need 300 ml of milk, 100 grammes of sugar, four eggs, two tablespoonfuls of potato flour and a little vanilla. Boil the milk, sugar and vanilla. Take off the heat and let it cool. Dilute part of the potato flour in a tablespoonful of water. Slowly stir in the rest, mixing gently to obtain a smooth paste. Add a pinch of salt. Place on a hot flame and continue to stir until the paste thickens. Set it to cool.

Add the egg yolks, then fold in the whites, whisked into a firm froth. Pour into a deep (1.1-litre) dish, only half filling it, for the soufflé doubles during cooking. Cook for twenty minutes in a moderate oven, being careful not to keep opening the oven door to see how the dish is developing.

After dessert, it is time for coffee, offered with a liqueur – walnut *eau-de-vie*, perhaps. Usually I pompously quote the philosopher Michel de Montaigne, 'My last drink is always my largest', and order another glass of red Bergerac. And I let someone else drive home.

Measurements and Metric Conversion

Measurements have been given as they would be found when buying food in France, in grammes and millilitres. Often, when precise weight is not important, a spoon, teacup or wineglass would be used, and I have also used this approach as often as possible since it is so easy and practical. Spoonfuls are always level; for those who are worried, a teaspoon is equivalent to 5 ml and a tablespoon to 15 ml. Otherwise, the brief tables below should allow conversion of the weights and measures of food given in this book. Recipes are for four people unless otherwise specified.

METRIC TO STANDARD WEIGHTS

25 grammes	1 oz
50 grammes	2 oz
75 grammes	3 oz
100–125 grammes	4 oz
150 grammes	5 oz
175 grammes	6 oz
200 grammes	7 oz
225 grammes	8 oz
250 grammes	9 oz
275 grammes	10 oz
300 grammes	11 oz
325–350 grammes	12 oz
375 grammes	13 oz
400 grammes	14 oz

425 grammes	15 oz
450 grammes	1 lb
700 grammes	1½ lb
900 grammes	2 lb
1.4 kilos	3 lb
1.8 kilos	4 lb
2 kilos	4½ lb

METRIC TO LIQUID MEASURES

25 ml	1 fluid oz
50 ml	2 fluid oz
75 ml	3 fluid oz
100–125 ml	4 fluid oz
150 ml	5 fluid oz
175 ml	6 fluid oz
200 ml	7 fluid oz
225 ml	8 fluid oz
250 ml	9 fluid oz
275–300 ml	10 fluid oz
500 ml	18 fluid oz
575–600 ml	20 fluid oz
1 litre	35 fluid oz

FAHRENHEIT TO CENTIGRADE AND GAS OVEN TEMPERATURES

225°F	110°C	¼ Very cool
250°F	130°C	½ Very cool
275°F	140°C	1 Cool
300°F	150°C	2 Cool
325°F	170°C	3 Moderate
350°F	180°C	4 Moderate
375°F	190°C	5 Fairly hot
400°F	200°C	6 Fairly hot
425°F	220°C	7 Hot
450°F	230°C	8 Very hot
475°F	240°C	9 Very hot

Further Reading

J. Bentley *A Guide to the Dordogne*, Viking, New York 1985.

M. and S. Brown *Food and Wine of South-West France*, Batsford, London 1980.

R. Chapoullié *Le Périgord*, B. Arthaud, Paris 1954.

J.-P. Chavent *Le Périgord*, Solar, Paris 1976.

Chroniqueur du Périgord et du Limousin, Auguste Boucharie, Périgueux 1853–1856.

A.-M. Cocula-Vaillières *Un Fleuve et des Hommes. Les Gens de la Dordogne au XVIIIe siècle*, J. Tallandier, Paris 1981.

P. Delfaud 'La population et l'emploi,' *Revue économique du Sud-Ouest*, année 30, nos 3–4, pp. 7–37, Bordeaux 1981.

G. Delluc, J. Lagrange and B. Pierret *Le Périgord noir*, Éditions de lettres périgordines, Périgueux 1967.

La Dordogne et sa Région – Fleuve – Histoire – Civilisation, Fédération Historique du Sud-Ouest, Éditions Bière, Bordeaux 1959.

'Dordogne, patrimonie historique,' *Vieilles Maisons françaises*, no. 3, pp. 1–93, Paris 1982.

A. Escoffier *Ma Cuisine*, E. Flammarion, Paris 1934.

G. Fayolle *La Vie quotidienne en Périgord an temps de Jacquou le Croquant*, Hachette, Paris 1977.

P. Fénelon *Le Périgord*, Éditions Privat, Toulouse 1982.

J.-L. Galet *Connaissance de Périgueux*, Pierre Fanlac, Périgueux 1982.

P. Gascar *Terres de Mémoire. Gascogne, Guyenne, Quercy, Périgord noir*, J.-P. Delarge, Paris 1980.

Gastronomie 84. Périgord, Éditions R. Dessagne, Limoges 1984.

Z. Guignaudeau-Franc *Les Secrets des Fermes en Périgord Noir*, Berger-Levrault, Paris 1980.

ed. C. Higounet *Recherches sur l'histoire de l'occupation du Sol en Périgord*, Éditions de CNRS, Paris 1978.

ed. A. Higournet-Nadal *Histoire du Périgord*, Éditions Privat, Paris 1983.

O. L. Huften *The Poor of Eighteenth-Century France, 1750–1789*, Oxford University Press, Oxford 1979.

J. Law *Dordogne*, Macdonald, London 1981.

J. Maubourget *Choses et Gens du Périgord*, Librairie Floury, Paris 1941.

——*Domme et pays dommois*, Pierre Fanlac, Périgueux 1973.

——*Le Périgord Méridional des origines a l'an 1370*, A. Coueslant, Cahors 1926.

La Mazille *La Bonne Cuisine du Périgord*, E. Flammarion, Paris 1929.

H. Miller *The Air-Conditioned Nightmare*, Heinemann, London 1962.

P. Oyler *The Generous Earth*, Hodder and Stoughton, Sevenoaks 1950.

——*Sons of the Generous Earth*, Hodder and Stoughton, Sevenoaks, 1963.

A. Penton *Customs and Cookery in Périgord and Quercy*, David & Charles, Newton Abbot 1973.

Le Périgord, Richesses de France, Paris 1954.

Population par commune de 1876 à 1962, Département de la Dordogne, Institut National de la Statistique et des Études Économiques, Bordeaux, 1964.

Regards sur L'Économie de la Dordogne au seuil des années 80, Association Périgourdine d'Action Culturelle, Périgueux 1981.

J. F. Revel *Culture and Cuisine: A Journey Through the History of Food*, tr. Helen R. Lane, Doubleday, New York 1982.

G. Rocal and P. Balard *Science de Gueule en Périgord*, Éditions du Folklore, Saint-Saud, Dordogne 1938.

E. Le Roy *L'Année Rustique en Périgord*, Les Éditions du Périgord noir, Périgueux 1965.

——'La Belle Coutelière', in *Au Pays des Pierres*, Les Éditions du Périgord noir, Périgueux 1966.

——*Jacquou le Croquant*, Pierre Fanlac, Périgueux 1966.

J. Secret *La Dordogne de L'Auvergne au Bordelais*, Horizons de France, Paris 1962.

P. N. Stearns *Old Age in European Society: The Case of France*, Croom Helm, London 1977.

S. Steen *Caves of the Moon*, Victor Gollancz, London 1954.

E. Weber *Peasants into Frenchmen: The Modernization of Rural France 1870–1914*, Chatto and Windus, London 1979.

F. White *Three Rivers of France: Dordogne, Lot, Tarn*, Faber and Faber, London 1952.

K. Wood *The Other Château Country. The Feudal Land of the Dordogne*, John Lane the Bodley Head, London 1931.

Index

*Recipes are listed in the index; general topics discussed appear
on the contents page*